D1202669

HOW TO START, MAINTAIN AND EXPAND AN ASTROLOGICAL PRACTICE

Contributing authors to this text include: Chris McRae, David Cochran, Georgia Stathis, Maureen Ambrose, Michael Munkasey, Rick Levine, Robert P. Blaschke, Ray Merriman, Joanne Wickenburg, Mark McDonough, Arlan Wise, and Carole Devine.

Cover design: Fractal Graphics by Martha Ritchey & PEK (Dave Peck)

Published by *The Organization for Professional Astrology*, P.O. Box 9237, Naples, FL 34101, www.professional-astrology.org, in association with L.A.B. Professional Publishing, P.O. Box 4130, Woodbridge, VA 22194, www.labpublish.com.

ISBN: 0-9700696-2-6
Printed in the USA

INTRODUCTION

This book was born when OPA's earlier organizational form, PROSIG, first began in 1989. Our purpose for forming an organization was to have a forum for discussing issues which affected the lives of professional astrologers. At the time, these concerns weren't being addressed by any astrology group. We collected our thoughts, experiences, and hopes as we started our newsletter, "The Career Astrologer." It became obvious that much of our common ground formed a pool of knowledge on how an astrological practice should be run. We were, and are, concerned about how astrologers earn a living. We also wanted to set down some helpful guidelines for anyone wishing to become an astrologer. This manual was to serve this function.

Any profession needs some kind of structured career path. This requires some form of systematic education. After all, you can't have a real profession without a standardized method of training. As astrologers, we recognized that material on how to run an astrological practice was very minimal, almost non-existent.

Technical education in astrology made significant strides forward all through the second half of the twentieth century. However, training in the business side of astrology was seriously lacking. As a consequence, people could become very fine technical astrologers without having any idea of how to earn a living with their knowledge. But, without a way to earn a living, we never would have professional astrologers, thus no profession.

We wrote this book so that people would have some systematic guideline about how to earn a living as a professional astrologer. The general public has always been willing to pay for astrology. However, the type of astrology they consume, for the most part, isn't what we mean by astrology. Entertainment astrologers earn a living in astrology, but serious professional astrologers strive to have their work valued at a deeper more meaningful level. This is our vision; this is our goal. It is our hope that we practice our profession with enough dignity and conscience that we help the general public yearn for higher standards in the astrological work they consume. "How to Start, Maintain, and Expand an Astrological Practice" is a contribution toward realizing this goal.

You can't have a profession without people having a way to get training in the profession. Education takes several stages of development in astrology. Acquiring and testing basic astrological knowledge is an essential pre-requisite for all of us; i.e. we need to know the mechanics of how an astrological chart is constructed and have a reasonable method for interpreting it for a client. We assume you already have this training or are in the process of acquiring it. This work does not even address the issue of all the necessary mathematical, astronomical, interpretive, and consulting skills needed to do competent astrology. Although we all agree that anyone wishing to practice astrology as a career needs to have proven technical proficiency, there is still a battery of required skills the astrologer (or would-be astrologer) needs in order to have a satisfying life. This book is aimed at addressing the additional business savvy that each of us must learn in order to have a fulfilling career.

Also, on the other side of the equation, the general public looking for competent, honest astrologers has often been left without a clue as to where to go or how to find one. Teaching competent astrologers how to earn a living through their skills is part of developing a better astrology in our society.

For all the limitations, technical astrology education had been coming along for many years. Still, it's fair to say, until our organization took it up, there was no education for how one should or could practice astrology as a line of work.

The first edition of this book appeared in 1991. It was an attempt to gather together in one place our collective knowledge of how the person studying astrology could translate their knowledge into a livelihood. In 1992, we published a second edition, which expanded the material somewhat. For the next nine years this book wasn't re-edited or reissued, mainly because we, as an organization, were focused on other more urgent issues. Also, the project always seemed to be lacking some key components. When Carole Devine volunteered to gather and edit the writings of our authors coming into OPA's 2001 conference, this new edition took final shape.

This third edition of the manual represents a gigantic step forward. It is more practical and comprehensive than the earlier editions. If you notice something that is missing from this work, please let us know. The authors who have contributed to this work are simply the best in the world on the particular subject about which they are writing. This is why we asked them to contribute to this work. The field of astrology is changing so dramatically right now that new material will be collected and added for new editions with some frequency.

Those of us in OPA involved in the writing, always intended this book to be a real "How to.." Manual. We always wanted it to be practical, giving step-by-step instructions for how to open a practice, how to locate sources of income, how to advertise and market a practice, how to overcome the difficulties of being self-employed, how to design an office, how to establish good business practices, how to use community resources, how to work with other astrologers, how to contribute to the astrological community, and so forth. If you find help in this book, we have been successful. Join us in developing an easier career path for astrologers.

Yours For A Better Astrology,
Bob Mulligan
President of OPA
941-261-2840
bobmulliga@aol.com

TABLE OF CONTENTS

MARKETING AND BUILDING YOUR PRACTICE

PART ONE

by Georgia Stathis

Introductory Remarks

There is never really a "time" when any of us are truly ready to become astrologers. It can be more readily described as an urge or a call. There is always doubt as to whether or not we can do a great job.

If you have studied a long time and have passion for this material, then it might be most promising to simply plunge in slowly by working with your friends or acquaintances that might request your help. In time, when you receive feedback about your work, you will begin to understand how you work, in which areas you do well and which areas need developing. You must, however, foremost and always, regard yourself as a professional.

Mindset

One of the first things you need to realize, if you are going to be a professional astrologer, is that you are in business. When people ask you what you do, you tell them, "I am a professional astrologer".

I remember years ago when I first started studying astrology, my very first teacher was Jean Mulgrew, a gifted psychic astrologer. She probably wasn't any more than five feet tall in her stocking feet, but every time we were out together or at a party or other occasion and someone asked her what she did for a living, she stood very tall and told them that she was "a professional astrologer"!

I always watched the reaction on their faces as they asked this, then, very loaded question, but inevitably they would respond with quiet respect. I always remembered that lesson.

Basic Rules

The next remarks are a bit elementary, but they need to be covered in order to develop the above mindset.

If you are the type of person who has a hard time setting limits, then you really need to look at how you can develop that skill if you are going to work with clients.

Clients don't need advice...they need information. They may want you to give them the answers. All you can do is explain what happens when certain things in the sky hit certain things in peoples' charts.

In time, as you develop your consulting style, you will develop certain stories or motifs that are continually used in your work. By telling stories you make a point with clients.

We are here to help others. We are in the "helping professions." But we also need to set limits with clients, and it begins with the first appointment.

Specialization

You will notice that you find yourself drawn to certain specializations. There are many branches of astrology: horary, mundane, electional, synastry...the list goes on and on. There will be certain areas in which you excel or prefer, and these are the areas that should be where you focus your marketing efforts.

As you develop your specialization, your peers, as well as the public, will become aware of you. You won't be just an "astrologer" who can do different things. Your role will be more defined and therefore, more marketable. You might even be one of the folks who pioneer a new specialization that we do not have yet. Now that we have that down, let us talk about building your practice.

Building a Clientele

Your "farm" (as we used to call it in real estate) of potential clients is in every place you look. The most obvious and immediately supportive people are the acquaintances you have developed through your other businesses or school associations, particularly if they have been aware of your interest in astrology.

A way to start with these folks is to offer them little "mini" readings that can be of use to them either in person or on tape, and if they want to pursue it, they can call you for an appointment.

As you branch out and people hear about your work you will be sent referrals. There are always a few wonderful people that God puts on this earth that are wonderful mouthpiece-type net workers, and they'll tell everyone about you and your work. It might be a good idea as you build your clientele to give these special referral people a gift of a free session to show your appreciation of their support over the years.

Another way to "throw the dice" at building your client base is when you pay your bills. Once in a while put your business card in the same envelope with your payment. See what happens.

When people ask you what you do for a living, regardless of whether you have another job, first tell them you are developing your practice as a professional astrologer, particularly if you do not intend to stay with your current profession. It takes a lot of guts to tell people this, because the response may vary. Many years ago, it was particularly uncomfortable to tell people what you did, because it was not accepted, or, as my first teacher used to say, "we used to be weird; now we're interesting!"

Soon you'll develop a sense as to whether or not you should tell certain people what you do. If you run into someone who has an adamant stance against what you do, then back off. Do not try to confront or change their mind. Be familiar with the refrains and references that they might make. For example, the Bible and its many passages that "criticize" astrology is often referenced. There was a wonderful book addressing this written by Moby Dick several years ago entitled, *Astrology's Pew in Church*, and is still available through his son Jayj Jacobs' group, Experience Astrology, in San Francisco, California.

Setting Appointments

There are some very specific things you need to know unflinchingly before a client is to call. How long your sessions are, where you read, if you do phone readings, what your fee is, and which days you work.

When you answer the call, first ask who referred them and keep that name as part of the record that you keep for this client. If it is a referral, it develops as a much easier transaction.

When they call, you need to ask them what they want out of the consultation (I try not to use the word 'reading'). Is there more of a focus on the personal or the professional? (Don't spend too much time on the phone answering their questions before they ever walk through your door). Then tell them, "Let me tell you how I work. This is what I do (natal, progressions, etc), I am available_____(when), and my fee is _____." "When are you available?" Give them two dates for possibilities. "I have such-and-such a date and time

4

available or such-and-such a date and time; which would you prefer?"

Notice how all the questions are open-ended. This keeps the conversation open, particularly if there are issues around your fee. When they commit to an appointment, ask for their address and phone number as well as their birth information so that you can send them a clear set of directions and also calculate their chart. Do tell them your "cancellation policy" at this time, so they take you seriously.

When they give you their birth information, impress upon them the absolute importance of a birth time and that if it isn't right, you cannot do the best possible work for them. Repeat the birthdata to them over the phone to make sure that it is accurate, and again repeat it to them when you sit down to work with them.

If they are non-referrals, it is always a good idea to ask for a small deposit toward the work you will be doing prior to their appointment. This insures that they are serious and that your efforts are not wasted.

The day before their appointment call to confirm their time with you. It is very important that you have a reliable answering machine or voicemail that can answer your calls when you are away from the phone. It might also be a good idea to have a different phone line installed for your business, so you can maintain some semblance of privacy from clients as your business grows. Deduct all of the expenses.

It is not a good marketing idea to use an answering service. Why? Because answering service operators have good days and bad days, and the first impression that your potential client has when they call you will be the lasting impression. The person answering the phone needs to be consistently interested in the client, helpful and service-oriented. That is why a machine and voicemail work well. It is always consistent. If they don't leave a message, then the phone call wasn't that important anyway.

An answering machine also gives you more control over screening the calls so that you can devote yourself to your client work. Make sure to purchase an answering machine that has remote capabilities so that if you start traveling as an astrologer, you can call in for your messages. Checking voicemail remote is a snap, too.

In the beginning, you may have to see a lot of clients at night as you are building your practice, but as you become more established, you will be able to work a normal workweek with normal hours.

Fees

There will be many people who will not want to pay your fee or pay at all. If you are trying to build a paying practice, you need to clarify your issues around value and money and be clear about your fees and whether you are willing to barter services.

You may want to set your fees lower at the outset of your practice. Do a market survey comparing fees charged in your area. Do not undercharge!!

You need to do a breakdown of your costs and expenses to see what you are really making per hour. There is a wonderful book in paperback called, *Running A One-Person Business* written by Whitmyer, Rasberry, and Phillips and published by Ten Speed Press, Berkeley, California. This book takes you through the breakdown of what your costs are and what you should be charging.

You need to think about what your preparation time is, because that is part of your fee. At this point in my work, I am very clear that I charge a per hour fee, which must also apply to the preparation time, since I feel more comfortable with comprehensive prep time of two hours.

Everything counts, the amount of Xerox copies you make, your phone bill, and your printing costs. You need to keep accurate records to make this assessment. (More on this in the section entitled Record Keeping.)

You also need to value your work as an astrologer. You know that astrology is a wonderful tool because it gave you such insight into yourself and others.

After you have made these assessments, then set a fee. Remember to include regular cost of living increases and to charge according to expertise. As you become more skilled your service will be more valuable.

Building a Public Image

It is important to set a standard about yourself and your work from the beginning. You need to know if this is going to be a hobby, a half-job for extra income, or your profession. You need to know how you wish to come across. Eventually, you want to know the type of clientele you wish to develop.

If you have decided that you want to be very public, then you need to develop a public image by doing certain things. Once you are aware of your image, you should design, even if quite simple, an information sheet about your work, or if there is more in your budget, a brochure.

Before you design this, look at different brochures. What is it you like about them and do not like about them? Which ones draw you in, and which ones put you off? Perhaps you'll want to think about designing a logo that you can put on all your public relations material that gives you a look of co-ordination.

These days, it might be better do something more contemporary and clean in its look, with some suggestion about what you do, but lots of stars, crystal balls, hocus pocus looking drawings may put people off. You have to remember that people are reserved in their view of anything "new age", and the wrong drawing may push them away. Once you have decided this, make sure you list just a few things like a bit about your background, the major services you offer, how those services can BENEFIT them, and your phone number or fax number. DO NOT LIST AN ADDRESS IF YOU WORK AT HOME. If you work in an office, then you may.

Your business card should be coordinated with your information sheet or brochure. Vertical cards tend to stand out better than horizontals, and plain black or distinct colors on a simple white or off white background seem to work the best. The paper quality is a big factor, too. If it is a better paper, then it presents a better quality appearance.

If you have moved or relocated, DO NOT SCRATCH OUT YOUR PHONES OR ADDRESSES. This looks tacky. Get new cards printed.

If you have gone so far as to design a letterhead, place the address across the bottom, so that if you move, you can have your printer print a black strip across the address that looks like part of the design and reprint a new address and phone line.

Lectures

In each community, usually at the local Chamber of Commerce, there is available to the public a Directory of Organizations or the labeled addresses for these organizations. These service clubs are always looking for a free speaker to speak at their meetings. Usually these meetings are breakfast, lunch or dinner meetings and they allow you twenty minutes to speak. They will feed you, but they will not pay you.

You can, however, use this as a platform to get the word out about what you do. Just remember, when you are invited to speak to a group, that you give them some concrete benefits of why astrology might be of use to them and some stories of how it has worked for other clients you know.

Admittedly, these groups are a bit more difficult because they may view you as the entertainment for their meeting, but if you can keep it simple, concrete and to the point and allow time for questions, you can be quite effective.

You may only get one person out of each group as a client, but remember they are the "seed" for their group and it does take time. Some people may call you years later when they heard you speak only once.

To procure a speaking engagement, simply write a letter to their program director giving a bit about your background and what you do. If there are any newspaper articles about you, enclose a Xerox copy and tell them you are available for speaking. When you go to speak, set a standard of dress that presents you as a public person.

Always bring your materials to distribute and invite them to give you their business card if they wish to be on your mailing address. Sometimes, if you feel like it, you can get all their business cards and draw one name and gift them a session or 50% off on a session or whatever. When they call to ask you to speak, screen the program director. If it is a Christmas luncheon where there might be a lot of drinking, you might want to ask to speak at another time. Why? Because by the time they stop drinking, you may be invited to speak two hours later to a group that is not very clear!! Tell the program director what your parameters are – how long you can stay. Ask them when it begins and ends. Confirm the day or two before the event.

"BUT I'M SCARED TO DEATH TO SPEAK TO GROUPS!" A number of years ago, the first *Book of Lists* was published, and amongst the lists, there was one that indicated peoples' greatest fears. It was found that the number one fear was speaking in front of groups. Death fell somewhere around the seventh number! In other words, people would rather die than speak!

IS THAT HOW YOU FEEL?

Well, if you plan to be a working astrologer, you are going to be doing a lot of speaking. This can help you practice, and you can get some fun, yet affordable help that will teach you to deliver your individual or group message. Toastmasters International is available for both men and women in most cities. It is a fun, affordable weekly meeting, that gets you up on your feet for just a few seconds or minutes a week for an assigned speech.

In addition to the community organizations, you can talk to your local adult education facilities or recreation and parks departments. They may let you teach classes in astrology in the various cities surrounding you. They do the promotional work, and you just show up to teach. This is another way of getting yourself known.

You can send letters to your clients requesting speaking engagements to their groups like the women's networks or soroptomists. These are also excellent places in which to speak, because you already know some of the people in the audience.

House Parties

If you are first starting out, you can send letters, with a promotional flyer enclosed, to clients telling them that you can make available to them a kind of "house" party. You set the limit of how many people should be there, and make it the responsibility of the party coordinator to get the attendees' accurate birthdata. Then when you get there, you read each chart for only 5 to 7 minutes to the individual in front of their group. If they want more, they can make an appointment at a later date.

The host or hostess receives a full session, that he or she may use or pass on to a friend, as a gift from you for doing this.

Become Your Own Public Relations Firm

When you are giving an interesting lecture or event in the community, send the local newspapers a black and white velox of yourself (3 x 5 works well) and a press release on a news release form. Just a paper with "News Release" as a large heading will suffice.

In the first line, you tell them the five w's--who, what, why, where, and when. The rest is more information on your event. You make sure you start the news release with the city and state from which you are sending it.

For example:

PLEASANT HILL, CA--On Mar 15 2001, Georgia Stathis, local professional astrologer, will be speaking at the Sustainers Group of the Junior League. Her topic will be "Mid-Life Transitions and the Outer Planets." This event will begin at 7:00 p.m. at such and such address. For more information, call so and so at (925) 689-STAR or (925) 689-7827...

Follow-Up

Once you begin to build your mailing list, it might be a good idea to send out a quarterly or monthly newsletter to all your clients. This can be a simple number – 2 pages minimum. Inside of it include a mini overview for such things as the different signs and a forecast. Perhaps an overview of some of the greater cycles might be an idea. You name it. The purpose of this newsletter is not only to give your client some useful information, but to also promote some of your classes or specials. It is also a great way to keep in touch.

As your mailing list grows and there gets to be too many to whom send newsletters, you can begin a subscription only newsletter and get a bulk mailing permit from the post office that will allow you to send 200 or more for a lower postage rate.

As you develop your database and get more and more of your clients' birthdates, you can either design a computerized rating system or use one of the more popular database programs to pull these birthdates out of the database. Then make labels that you put onto birthday cards that are very lovely, but also have a gift of 20 to 30% off any fees and services you offer during their birthday month. This keeps you in touch with clients and invites them to use your services at a gifted rate, something people appreciate in these times. This also keeps a regular client flow going throughout the year so that you have a more precise projection of what income you might expect so that you can stick to your business budget.

There is one postcard promotion that I used to do entitled the "Timer Special", where you send postcards out to clients. They state that you are making available to them sessions for 25 or 35 minutes clocked by the timer. You set it up to sound like a fun thing to do that is a "budget special". The postcard is worded like a game – "25 for 25", and the "rules" are that when the timer is up, their time is up, unless they want to contract for more time at your regular rate. The postcards usually have a time frame in which the individual can use them. They are also less expensive to mail.

You can use postcards for other things too. Announcements, invitations to an office open house, gift certificates, new services or report writers that might be available. Again, it is another way to keep your name in front of your clients. Remember, don't let anything leave your office that does not look professional. First impressions are often both first and last! A great website for pre-printed postcards is www.modernpostcards.com.

Equipment

Anyone starting out does not need a lot of equipment to be an astrologer. In the time of Ptolemy, all they had were their brains, books and writing utensils. However, we have come a long way as astrologers and are quite fortunate to be growing up in the computer age, and the computer is the perfect tool for any astrologer. This is primarily because of the accuracy a computer offers.

It is important, if you can, to have a computer with enough software that allows you to not only calculate astrological charts, but also serves as a word processor for letters, announcements, and mailing label producer, so that you can send out materials that are useful to your clients.

If you don't have a computer, at least have a good typewriter, or access to one, as well as a reliable answering machine that sounds good and is consistently operative. There is nothing more frustrating to an individual calling you for an appointment than to be cut off or not recorded. Remember, if you lose them once, they may not call back.

It is not necessary when you first start out to supply the client with a taped recording of the session. Although, as your practice grows, it may be a good investment to have a clear and succinct-sounding tape recorder and supply them with courtesy tapes that you do not guarantee.

Down the road, you might want to get a Xerox machine or fax if you do a lot of mailing or long distance work.

Record Keeping

There are two different schools of thought on this one. One is to not keep any records at all so that when the client comes in, each time things are fresh. That is not my school of thought, and as far as storage goes, I do pay the price! I keep records of my clients' charts, transits, progressions, as well as

13

particularly earthshaking events in their lives for future review when they come in yearly.

The other reason I keep these records is that it affords the client an opportunity to call during the year for a short session on the phone if something really needs attention. They know you have their information, and they depend on you keeping it because a lot of people do not remember birth times. If you have it handy, you will not lose them when they call.

Every few years, if you haven't seen a client, you can go through and sweep your files, but only if you haven't seen them in awhile.

Generating Other Income

It would be wonderful if we could simply make our living doing client work, but anyone who has done it for some time knows that it is grueling. If you intend to make this your profession, you need to consider other avenues that are part of astrology. This could be making available to clients report writers like the many that are available through ASTROLABE, KEPLER, A.I.R.S. Software, MATRIX, ASTRODATABANK, HALLORAN, and many more.

When properly marketed through birthday specials, or four for such-and-such special price promotions, these products can generate some passive income, so that you can either spend more time working with your clients' charts or developing other products like lectures or books.

They say that variety is the spice of life, and this is very true in the world of astrology. As communicators, we need more than one vehicle of expression to keep ourselves fresh. If you find that you are a particularly gifted speaker, you can develop that skill, and then produce and sell tapes of your lectures as a service to clients or others who want to learn more about astrology or astrological techniques.

You can teach beginning, intermediate, and advanced classes in astrology. You can teach special workshops on one particular avenue of astrology. By doing this, you cultivate a following of students who will stay with you if you have interesting information to offer them.

Re$ale Licenses

If your speaking or teaching sessions grow, you might want to consider selling tapes to students. You can get a resale license from your STATE BOARD OF EQUALIZATION, which allows you to purchase books and tapes at a wholesale price and sell the same books and tapes to clients or students for the full retail price. This entails some type of record keeping system because you do pay the resale tax each year. Usually you pay a wholesale price that is 60% of the retail price. You can write books or more simply, articles, for your local paper, advertiser, etcetera, that can act as good publicity for you, too.

Taxes

Briefly, declare what you make. One group you do not want to fool with is the government. I have always declared all of my income, not only for tax purposes, but also if I ever want to get a loan for a new piece of equipment or to enlarge my business, there is a record. The government knows me as a consultant. That is all they need to know.

As a self-employed individual, you will be required to file a quarterly Estimated Tax. Because of this, it is important to keep records of all expenses and income. As a self-employed individual, you can have your tax person help you set up a self employed pension plan that you pay into each year at tax time, that will help whenever, if ever, you decide to retire. It is also a way of deferring some of the tax you owe each year. Instead of paying the government, you pay yourself something.

Assistants

They are gold!!!!! Once your practice starts building, there comes a time when you shouldn't be doing certain things, like monthly mailings or taking your own appointments. Why? Because you won't have time and a good assistant can lend support to your client and yet shield you, too, so that you can focus on your work.

You don't need to have an assistant full-time; they can work for you part-time. It also lends a degree of credibility to your work if you have someone other than yourself answering the phone. They don't have to know astrology, but a little bit of astrological knowledge seems to make the job easier on the assistant.

Giving Back

Give something back to the community in which you work in time or service. Provide a sliding scale or occasional gifts for selected individuals that you feel might really need assistance at a certain time.

Occasionally, you will hear one of your clients tell you that another one of your clients is having a hard time financially, and they want to gift that client with a session with you, but they know the client wouldn't like it. What I do for that one is tell them about my system, "CLIENT OF THE MONTH"! I make up a postcard that is written as a winning raffle card, and the first client sends me the money for the session. I send a postcard to the client who really needs a session, but is too proud to ask for one. The postcard says, "Congratulations, you are the winner of THE CLIENT OF

THE MONTH AWARD! You get a free session with Georgia." It works every time, and everybody turns out happy.

Also, give back to your community by purchasing a business license. I always purchase a license as a consultant and let it go at that. That way no one can say I do not have a license. It also keeps you abreast of what is going on in your community and city hall.

Conclusion

Basically, marketing your practice consists of three things:

1. SALES
2. STRUCTURED PROCEDURES
3. FOLLOW-UP

The same is true in any sales and marketing situation. Yes, it seems like a lot of work, but this business, like any other business, thrives on consistency. Establishing procedures and set practices helps you stay focused as an astrologer so that you can do the best possible work. WORK? Did I say work? To this day after twenty- five years, it still feels like PLAY and I love it. Best of luck to you in your new endeavors as professional astrologers!!

PART TWO

Marketing and Building Your Practice with Technology

Those comfortable with various forms of media may want to consider investing the resources to connect their computer databases to a built-in modem fax/phone and web site. A built-in modem enables your computer to talk to other computers and fax machines worldwide. This handy feature allows you to press a few buttons to send fax blasts and emails to all of your customers saving you both printing costs and TIME!

So what can that do? How about announcing a sale? 10% off all consultations booked the week of October 15- 22? Boom! All of your customers know this TODAY. Any HOT NEWS that you want to share with your customers can be done with absolute ease. Technology was meant to streamline human efforts and computers can if you are willing to spend the necessary set-up time.

The same is true for developing and maintaining a web site. In all areas of the world you can create your own web site and have it "hosted", meaning you pay another site for access or hire someone to create and maintain a site for you. Costs vary depending on how many bells and whistles you add. The benefits? Customers find you!!!!

Think of it as a giant yellow page set. If you have built key word links to your site, anyone looking for the words URANUS or ASTROLOGY or ASTROLOGERS or PISCES will automatically be given an option to review your site. This is a very visual and creative medium. Meaning you can appeal to a wide audience. You can opt to attach your web site to an existing independent bookstore's site, or any other business that complements yours, to save even more money. By adding to an existing site you avoid the hosting fees, which can add up.

Other gadgets that may make your life easier are palm pilots that hot sync to your computer. What does that mean? If a customer tells you that they have changed their phone or address or any other critical information, you can input it into your hand-held computer and make the change instantly. The next time you use your computer you attach this gizmo to it, and it makes the update for you in your corresponding database. Sounds like too much work? Well if you have ever been at a conference where you run into a couple of dozen people thrusting their new business cards at you, you know the hassle of keeping track of those cards and then inputting it all when you get home. Much better to have the person give you the update on the hand-held.

Lastly, don't overlook your local media. They are always looking for interesting people to interview. If you should manage to get yourself onto a local radio or television program, or into the newspaper to promote your business, then in addition to giving your phone number, you can advertise your web site! Remember to put your web address on any piece of documentation that goes out, be it in a fax, email or on paper!

By thinking through all of the available forms of getting your message out, you'll soon be a marketing expert and your business will blossom!

* * * * *

Georgia Stathis has been a full-time professional astrologer since 1977. Her background in business which includes investments, real estate, and public relations, advertising and marketing, has been a base from which she draws and applies it in her private work as an astrologer for companies and individuals.

A well-loved lecturer, she was educated at Northwestern University in Chicago, Illinois where she received her B.S. degree in Communications and also at Pepperdine University in Malibu, California where she received her Masters in Business Administration degree (M.B.A.).

A former board member of ISAR, she is currently a member of the faculty of Kepler College of Astrological Arts and Sciences at Seattle, Washington. Featured in such publications as the London Economist and the Sacramento Bee of California, she has just completed a series of weekend Business Astrology Intensives.

Her publishing company, Starcycles, produces an annual timing book, the Starcycles Calendar (which uses astrological timing and is written in "English" for anyone to use), as well as over 100 tapes of lectures and classes available through her website at www.starcycles.com. Her brand new book, "Business Astrology 101: Weaving the Web Between Business and Myth" is now available by calling 1-866-781-7249 Toll Free.

PLANNING TIME AND SPACE

by Chris McRae, PMAFA, NCGR.CA, ISAR.CAP

Utilizing time and space efficiently and effectively are two important facets of being a successful astrologer or working for yourself in any business enterprise.

Planning Time

Initially, you should set two separate financial goals each of which involves using your time effectively. The first goal is to make enough money to pay your rent/mortgage and exist comfortably on a day by day, month by month basis. You will have to decide how much you need to charge and how many clients per week you need to see in order to meet that preliminary goal. The second goal is to make enough money to update your present equipment, take an annual vacation, and attend an annual or biannual conference in order to continually upgrade your education and receive valuable input from the astrological community at large.

In order to do this, it is mandatory that you determine your business hours and maintain a basic routine that can be altered as the need arises. It has often been said that people who reach income levels of 6 figures rise at least by 5:00 AM. Arnold Schwarzenegger gets up at 4:00 AM to do 2 hours of weight lifting. It is not difficult once you get used to it and if you have a reason. Early rising would give you time to exercise, sip your coffee, read the paper, answer both your E-Mail and paper mail, groom yourself, do client preparation, and be ready to see your first client at 8:30 or 9:00. Exercise is an important part of your daily routine because you will be spending much of your day sitting. Exercise not only tones your body, but it will stimulate mental activity and a good attitude. Reading the paper or listening to the morning news is also very important in order to keep abreast of what is happening in the world. This is essential in order to understand the background or social conditions surrounding your client's life. Answering your mail at the same time every morning sets up a routine and keeps it from accumulating and creating anxiety. Client preparation should also be done at a quiet time of the day when your phone isn't ringing. You may do this in the early morning, or you may choose to set aside a specific day for this work.

You also need time to be creative in order to increase your business, such as planning your monthly newsletter to your clients, sending out birthday greetings, upgrading or creating your website, approaching various community organizations on making a presentation. If you teach, you may need time to prepare class material. You need time to read newsletters from the organizations you belong to so you know what is happening in your own professional community. You need time to read articles on how to advance your business, gain publicity and learn new public relations techniques, gain media knowledge such as how to prepare and present press releases, etc.

The amount of effort and time you invest in all of the above will determine if and when you pass the magic income level of being able to barely meet expenses to being affluent. Of course, if you have a family surrounding you, and you are conducting a home-based business, your schedule must be adjusted accordingly.

Working for oneself has a major pitfall which involves the efficient and effective use of time. It is all too easy to sleep in, run out shopping on a whim, take care of morning domestic chores before getting to your business, saunter into your office when you feel like it, and spend the next hour talking with a friend on the phone. If you had an employer who expected you to be at your desk between specific hours, you would likely get fired if your personal life interfered with those obligations.

The same holds true if you are working for yourself. You might find it useful to consider *self* as your employer because if you don't pay attention to your business affairs adequately, you certainly will not get a pay cheque either.

You may find rising at 5:00 or 6:00 AM prohibitive because you see clients all evening. Personally, I do not. I feel I am entitled to a personal life with my family and friends. Other professionals do. When I am booking an appointment with a new client, after the preliminary conversation, I say, "my professional hours are from 9:00 to 5:00, what is best for you?" If they tell me they work and cannot be here during those hours, I suggest either an early morning, an extended lunch hour, or leaving work an hour early. They may also have a day off other than Saturday or Sunday and may be trying to save it for leisure activities or catching up on personal chores. I work too, and my work involves seeing clients. I have never lost a client due to my professional hours simply because I am always prepared to make a compromise. That leaves my evenings for teaching and enjoying a reasonable family or personal life. Occasionally I may have to book out of town clients on Friday evening or Saturday morning. Common sense prevails here. There are many ways to conserve time which we will not attempt to outline fully here. For instance, handle your mail only once. Do not let it accumulate on your desk and become part of a permanent pile or take hours to whittle down. It is useful to make a weekly goal of what you would like to achieve during the week and then break it into days. Everyday just before you leave your office, or before retiring for the evening, make a list of what you need to do tomorrow. If I don't do that, I find at least some valuable time slips through my fingers. What you do not complete today should go at the top of tomorrow's list. You might also wish to put the longest or least desirable task at the top. When that task is completed, it gives a great sense of achievement and seems to invigorate or add energy to the rest of the day. Many of these techniques are outlined in books or articles on time management. If you cannot find one at your local bookstore or library, phone a business college and ask for a title.

Planning Space

Some people are more conscious or inspired by their atmosphere than others. Your own office space should be first and foremost comfortable for you and aesthetically pleasing. After all, you spend a lot of time in it. In my own office, I have one wall in walnut paneling which is completely lined with book shelves neatly bulging with books. My desk space and computer work station occupy two other walls. The furniture is white and the carpet is a royal blue on hardwood. The floor space should contain at least two comfortable client chairs with a small low table or coffee table that can be shared by the occupants of both chairs. Some astrologers like to work side by side with their client but I like to be across from them so I can look easily into their eyes and judge every nuance of their expression and body language. A low table is not a barrier but gives you a little extra space between you and your client. I can lean towards them, pat them on the hand, or even get up and walk around to them if there is a need. In other words, your workplace should look like a working office, be relatively organized, and provide a private, quiet, comfortable place where your client can feel safe. You may need a door that closes, particularly if there is someone else in the house.

This concept would not vary much if you had an outside office in a professional building. However, in that case you would need a secretary/receptionist to welcome your clients, answer your phone and do your chart preparation. More and more people are working from home because it saves expensive downtown parking, gas, traffic irritation and lost time. These savings can be passed on to your clients. It also relieves them of potential parking problems. Some of this, of course, will depend upon where you live.

You must always be prepared for your client. It gives them a sense of security to know you care. I place their natal chart, three-wheel progressed chart, transit list or any other papers I may use, in front of my client, facing their direction. Many of them do not understand the charts or glyphs, but in time they develop a familiarity. It is graphic. It shows your client where you get the information. I also include a clean pad of paper and pen in case they wish to write something down. The session is taped so note taking is not necessary. I display my own papers on my side of the table. Your computer could be on and facing your client. Your client must feel they are expected and know you are prepared. I once had a client come to see me who said she had an appointment with an astrologer who came to the door pulling a sweater over her head, hair in disarray, and sleep in her eyes. She asked the client to wait until she ran the chart on her computer. Needless to say, I gained a new client and that astrologer lost one. She wonders why she is debt ridden and financially desperate. It appears little effort is put into being successful. It is never handed to us. We have to earn it.

When the session is over, I place his/her papers and tape in an 8-1/2 x 11 envelope. Otherwise your client will fold the papers and stuff them in a pocket or purse. At this point I rise, indicating the time is up, and I escort the client to the door.

You need to present a professional image from beginning to the very end if you wish to keep your clients and build a successful business.

* * * * *

Chris McRae is a full-time professional astrologer and teacher. She lectures at major conferences and travels internationally delivering weekend workshops for various astrological organizations. She has written two books, The Geodetic World Map and

Understanding Interceptions, and was a contributing author in the Llewellyn anthology series. Chris also hosted her own television talk variety shows and has guested countless times over many years on other shows espousing the virtues of astrology.

PREPARING FOR EACH CLIENT

by Maureen Ambrose

Preparation is everything. That's how one gets to Carnegie Hall. Preparation is a process needed for success; it's why people study a subject; it's the foundation of what we do well in life. Once we have made all those preparations that have brought us to the point of someone getting in contact with us to either inquire or contract for our work, we need to further prepare the potential client and ourselves for the consultation.

First of all, always be prepared with business cards on hand. If one is at a social gathering or other event, there is always the possibility of someone asking about your work or asking about making an appointment. Give them the card and ask them to call you for an appointment. If the person wants to know more about what you do, be prepared to speak generally about the kinds of services you have to offer. Know how you wish to describe your work and the terms you wish to use. Do you give a reading or consultation? Are these terms interchangeable? If you are asked about your fees, be ready to reply clearly concerning the time and different fees you may offer for particular kinds of work.

The Appointment

When someone calls for an appointment, it is necessary for you to "interview" that person to determine what he or she needs from you, the astrologer, during the reading. Be prepared to describe the various services you offer whether it is natal, financial, horary, medical, forecast updates, real estate, vocational, solar returns, locational, relationship, psychological or whatever direction your expertise includes. Be honest concerning what you can offer. You need to ask,

"What do you want from this reading, and why do you want it at this particular time?" This helps to start the framework to build the session around the client's most important concerns. The client becomes aware that you are interested in hearing what he or she has to say. All of this sets a tone and the goals for the session. Be clear about what you can and cannot accomplish during a single session. State disclaimers about your work now and during the actual session. Define your limits and boundaries. You must be clear about what you charge and the type of payment you accept.

Do you accept checks from a new client? Do you require a deposit from a new client? Do you accept credit card payments? If you have a cancellation policy, you must make this clear. If you don't have a cancellation policy as such, perhaps you might require a phone call from the client the day before to confirm the appointment. Ask potential new clients if they have had other astrological readings and by whom. Ask how they got your name? Was it by referral, then who? Was it by advertisement, then where? Note all these details on a client card or client folder. One of the best ways to insure that all these details will be communicated is to have a checklist of items you need to tell a new client who is phoning for an appointment. In that way either you or your office assistant can have this list handy to assure that all items are communicated.

As you listen to the client's story, acknowledge that you understand his or her needs and that you would be addressing these concerns during your meeting. This will put the client at ease knowing that their communication has been received and understood. Make sure that the client's concerns are recorded so that they are not overlooked later on. At this point you have likely sold the client on your work. If you have communicated a feeling of warmth and empathy, so much the better. It could help to relieve the client's feelings of anxiety if any are present.

You have learned about the client's expectations and whether you can meet them. These questions help both you and the client prepare for the appointment. For clients new to astrological work, they will have a better understanding of what can be accomplished at the session. Of course, it is your decision if you want this client or not. In some cases, you may not want to contract with this particular person. Perhaps this person's needs are unrealistic, and you cannot meet those expectations. In that case, neither one of you would be satisfied with the consultation. Perhaps the client will be needing a different professional to handle those needs. In fact the interview can screen out people who are very sick or disturbed. If this becomes apparent during the client interview, be prepared to have specific names to give as referral whether it would be for therapy, bodywork, doctor, suicide hotline or lawyer. If the person's needs would be better served by another astrologer for some specialty where you have insufficient expertise such as Astro*Carto*Graphy, horary, business, etc., then have referral names to suggest.

Try to be as concise as possible. However, don't forget to make the caller aware of your credentials and background to further put them at ease. Once you have covered all the necessary issues, and you determine that the caller's needs can be met, offer to set an appointment date. Once the date is selected, ask the caller about birth data. Be sure to determine if the source of the data is from a birth certificate or some official record. Ask the caller's full name and spelling, address and telephone number. Does the caller have a cell phone and business number as well? Ask if the client has an email address. Note these details on a client card for future reference. Ask the caller whether he or she is married, divorced, currently in a relationship, have children, is presently working and the kind of work that person does. Are parents living? Does the caller have siblings? Ask any other questions that you feel would help you frame activity in the person's life.

Next you need to supply the client with directions to your office. If you wish the client to bring a tape and tape recorder, mention this detail. If you will be taping the session for them, let the client know you will be providing this service. Before you end the call, repeat the date of the appointment and the birth data.

The Work

The first part of the client preparation has been completed. You have made a verbal contract with the client. The next step is preparing the charts for the consultation and scheduling the amount of time you routinely need to handle the work. Each astrologer develops a work style. The particular system utilized for the particular need of the session is accessed. Charts are prepared and studied. Notes are taken and a plan concerning the dialogue is clarified. The client's chart is analyzed concerning the issues discussed in the initial interview phone call. The chart is also analyzed for major aspect configurations. These represent important "red flags" in the client's life. These aspects will represent the challenges and growth experiences the client has needed. The challenges will continue until the person realizes what they are and what is needed to manage them. The time involved in this portion of the preparation varies greatly. Some astrologers work quickly with little preparation while others require several hours. The object is to be prepared according to your skill level and the manner in which you prefer to work. The more work you do, the faster you will be able to move through the chart preparation.

The Consultation Day

Earlier in the day before the client's appointment, review the chart(s) and notes you have made. Have them in your consciousness if necessary. Recall the concerns of the client. You may develop a ritual or routine you wish to perform prior to the client's arrival. This might include meditation or asking for guidance from some place of wisdom you access. Make sure that your office is attractive and properly arranged. Clear away any unnecessary papers, and provide a setting that is comfortable, clean and reflective of you. Some astrologers prepare a consultation chart for the time of the appointment, gathering additional information as to the nature of the meeting. You might want to experiment with this consultation chart to decide if this, too, is something you wish to include in your routine.

The time has come. The client is at your door. Greet this client with warmth and enthusiasm. Smile. This is a new relationship that may continue beyond today. This person has chosen you for a reason and you are there to provide them with some very valuable information. You are there to create light and illumination. You are a professional. Convey that message as you begin. Remember that first impressions count.

Adjustments

You have it made, right? Wrong! Always be open to make changes and adjustments to your routine if you feel that something else will work even better. For instance, you might want to consider putting your policies and methods into a printed statement and sending it to the client to read before the consultation.

This can be a very satisfactory way to prepare the client and clarify general questions before hand. Perhaps you want or need to make scheduling adjustments as your practice begins to grow and your schedule becomes more and more crowded. Are you able or willing to run sessions back to back? Are you prepared with a suitable waiting area for your next client? Do you need to create a way of discarding the mental frame from your work with one client as you begin a session with the next one? How do you handle other activities of the day? These are questions that might cause you to pause and reconsider your routine. As you do, you will be creating the operating style that works for you. You will be better able to manage your practice, enjoy your work and get more satisfaction from it. A good set of guidelines can help keep stress at a minimum and likely help you to be more successful at what you do. As your business grows, it will change and so will you. Consider yourself and your business a work in progress. Learn from your mistakes and keep a sense of humor about most things. A smile can be an important ingredient in your astrologer-client relationship. Be generous with your positive energy. It's good for both you and your client.

Summary
IN A FEW WORDS: Be Prepared

The Appointment
- Business cards are a must
- Interview the potential client
- Create a client profile
- Communicate your services
- Determine the client's needs
- Convey your price, time and other policies
- Are you the professional they require?

The Work
- Prepare the necessary charts
- Review the goals of the session

The Appointment
- Refresh mentally
- Check office environment
- Welcome the client
- Be your creative self

Further Adjustments
- How can you do it better?

* * * * *

Maureen Ambrose is an Advisory Board member of OPA. She is a former officer with ProSig. Presently she is an officer on the board of directors of ISAR. She is a former chapter president with NCGR and is an area representative for AFAN. She is Regulus Chairperson for the UAC conference schedule July of 2002. Maureen writes a regular column for The International Astrologer journal. She has been published in American Astrology magazine. An astrologer for well over 30 years, Maureen has a consulting practice, teaches, and lectures. She may be reached by email Mambroz@aol.com.

HOW A COUNSELING ASTROLOGER CAN BENEFIT FROM RESEARCH

by Mark McDonough

Introduction

Every student of astrology eventually hits "The Wall." The wall is inscribed with the question, "I've read all the basic books. They are all starting to repeat themselves. What do I do next to improve my astrological know-how?" At this point most people go exploring new or rediscovered techniques. We might add new points to the chart like asteroids, arabic parts, midpoints, fixed stars, etc., investigate more esoteric aspects like the quintiles and deciles, or learn whole new systems of interpretation like ancient or Vedic astrology. I would like to propose that the best way to deepen your astrological knowledge is through qualitative research.

In some sense, we do qualitative research every time we read a new chart. We are observing how a different combination of the archetypes combined with other factors like gender, race and level of consciousness changes the range of their expression. It is only through the detailed working out of the possibilities that we get to really know astrology. Textbooks point out the basic principles, but to deepen and extend our knowledge - to become better counseling astrologers - we have to study lots of charts.

Our understanding of astrology will become much deeper faster if we also study charts more systematically. By gathering charts with similar astrological factors and looking for common traits, we learn new things not found in textbooks. Similarly, by gathering charts with similar biographical traits

35

and looking for common astrological factors we will also gain a deeper appreciation for how astrology works.

Qualitative vs. Quantitative Research

Qualitative research:
§§   Generates "theories" from a small set of particular examples.
§§   Uses inductive logic - "There seems to be a common model behind this set of observations."
§§   Persuades through clarity of thought - "Does the argument make sense? Is it logically coherent?"
§§   Is best for learning new things.

Quantitative research:
§§   Starts with an hypothesis and tests it against data
§§   Uses deductive logic - "If this model is true, then I should observe the
    following."
§§   Persuades through counting - "Is there a statistically significant difference between the average count in the experimental and control group?"
§§   Is best for testing if what we "know" is reliable.

If we pull together a set of charts of people with arthritis and look for common astrological themes we are doing qualitative research. Let's suppose that we did this and found many hard aspects to Saturn. We would find the argument persuasive because Saturn rules bones, and hard aspects are considered problematic. We may consider this a new piece of astrological knowledge arising from a qualitative research study.

Now suppose we wanted to test this "theory" to find out how reliable it was. Then we would enter into the realm of quantitative research. We would gather a second set of charts and divide them into two groups: those that do suffer from arthritis and those that do not. We would count the number of hard aspects to Saturn in each group and perform a statistical test to find out if the difference in the number of hard Saturn aspects in each group was significant or not. The statistical definition of significance is based on probability. What is the probability that the difference between the two counts is just random luck? In social science research the luck factor has to be less than 5%. Given the incredible claim that planets actually affect people's lives, in astrological research we like to see a luck factor of less than 1%.

Notice the direction of our reasoning. We can go up from the data to form a model that correlated arthritis with hard aspects to Saturn. We then went back down into another set of data to test that model. On the way up we were persuaded by qualitative criteria that there was congruence between the model and other things we know about Saturn. On the way down we were persuaded by quantitative criteria that there was a statistically significant difference in the counts of hard aspects to Saturn in the experimental and control groups. Qualitative research generates new ideas; quantitative research tests them for reliability.

Qualitative Research into Fundamental Principles of Astrology

The entire body of knowledge that we call "Astrology" is founded on qualitative research. We know what we know from hundreds of generations of astrologers observing the skies and making inferences about their correspondence with human behavior. We used metaphor and analogy to guide the process of looking for correlations. We reasoned that the Sun was in Aries during the spring so Aries must have something to do with new beginnings. We built models like Earth, Air, Fire and Water plus Cardinal, Fixed and Mutable to give us a deeper understanding of the 12 signs and how they relate to each other. When the models told a consistent story we knew we were learning something.

We are still learning new things about astrology. We have seen more ideas introduced into the astrological corpus in the 20th century than in any previous century. Harmonics, midpoints, composite charts, astrocartography, depth psychology and asteroids are all recent ideas that have broadened and deepened our understanding of astrology. These "big ideas" are all born of intuitive leaps based on previous knowledge extended through inference and analogy.

Personally I am not a fan of the "yet one more interesting technique to look at" line of research. I think we have much more work to do in gaining a better understanding of our fundamental principles and how they interact.

Richard Tarnas' work on Uranus/Prometheus is a great example of research into one of our fundamental principles. His book, Prometheus the Awakener, is a deep study of the planet Uranus. When he studied the lives of revolutionaries, inventors and originators who had Uranus prominent in their chart, he found that their life stories had much more in common with the story of Prometheus than the story of Uranus. Along the way he provided many more metaphors for counseling astrologers to use in discussing Uranus problems in client charts.

Lois Rodden and I decided to take a new look at the archetypes of Fire, Earth, Air and Water by looking at the lives of people who were extraordinarily high or low in each element. Looking at extreme examples to understand fundamental principles is a well-trod path in qualitative research. Psychologists study the severely mentally ill to get a clearer picture of the psychological processes that drive the merely neurotic. The dynamics are similar, only toned down in the neurotics. Similarly in astrology we can understand the dynamics of the archetypes better if we study the charts of extreme cases.

Please refer to www.astrodatabank.com/ASWater.htm for an example of this type of research

Qualitative Research into the Interaction of Archetypes

Have you noticed how little fresh writing there is in astrology today? Most of what's out there is a regurgitation of previous textbooks. The only way to get fresh insight is to be willing to do the work of diving into a sea of data. We need to see how the archetypes interact in real lives. We need to see how gender, race, class and level of consciousness change the range of expression.

I would like to see lots more research done on the highest and lowest expressions of the astrological archetypes. One of the games we like to play at the AstroDatabank booth is, "Tell us the least favorite aspect in your chart and we'll show you a number of famous people with that aspect. Then you can read their biography to find out how they dealt with it."

I think that the "highest and lowest" game is the core of the astrological reading. We speak to people about the core dilemmas and talents written in their chart. They sigh at feeling so deeply seen. We ask them questions about how the astrological dynamics are playing out in their life. Then we use our knowledge of the potential inside the archetypes to introduce them to a higher way of working out these dynamics.

One book that rises above the pack and tells us lots about the highest and lowest expressions found in the interactions of archetypes is Sue Tompkins' book *Aspects in Astrology*. Sue Tompkins is one of the very few authors who lists the sources for all her data in the back of the book. She lists six data books and the data for every famous person mentioned in the book. She has done her homework and it shows. This is top quality qualitative research rooted in thousands of charts of famous people and clients. It extends our knowledge of how the archetypes play out in real lives.

Donna Cunningham has also mined new ground in her brilliant series of articles for The Mountain Astrologer where she has studied contacts between Venus and the outer planets. See www.astrodatabank.com/ASVenusNeptune.htm for a reprint of her work.

Why We Need Quantitative Research

Qualitative studies are great for coming up with new techniques, exploring the archetypes more deeply and developing models for which astrological factors are correlated with which behavioral factors, but they can't be used to prove anything. Only quantitative techniques can tell us how reliable these techniques and models are. Until you start counting, the strongest truth one can claim is "It seems to me such and such is important.", but it is basically one philosopher's opinion against another's.

My image of contemporary astrology resembles that of Santa Claus staggering under a heavy bag full of toys. And Santa's bag keeps getting heavier as we invent or rediscover more ways to analyze the chart. Let me catalog the chaos. We have tropical and sidereal zodiacs, geocentric and heliocentric charts, three or four rulership systems, eight ways to progress a chart, 16 house systems, 20+ arabic parts, 78 or more midpoints, 180 levels of harmonics, 5000 asteroids, and now I hear we should start adding deep space objects to our charts.

Why do we have such a massive confusing mess of factors to deal with? Because there has been no way to toss anything out. Every technique works some of the time. You can always find five stunning examples of how the asteroid Winchester was involved in a shooting or how the tertiary progression predicted a bankruptcy to the day. But which are the techniques that work 80% of the time and which ones work only 30% of the time? Which ones are the fine-tuners that confirm major trends, and which ones are the basics that make up the fundamental structure of a reading. The only way we will find this out for sure is through research?

Many people claim that astrology is just too subtle and complex to yield to quantitative research. They claim that standard scientific research methods cannot handle the symbolic, meaning based, synchronistic reality that is at the core of astrology.

That's nonsense.

"As above, so below" is a statement about correlation and correlation is a core statistical concept. If we can't show a correlation between astrological and behavior factors, then there is no "below" that is "as above."

Our field is in desperate need of quantitative research to cut through the plethora of techniques that have been invented and rediscovered in the last 50 years. We had better be able to go beyond qualitative research if we ever want to adjudicate differences of opinion in astrology and start dealing with our rat's nest of house systems, zodiacs, rulerships, ayanamshas, orb sizes, progression systems, and so forth.

In order for us to have a breakthrough in quantitative astrological research we need better tools. We need to be able to teach computers to analyze charts in a way that mirrors the process a human astrologer goes through. The computer needs to be able to look at multiple factors at once, weighing them together and balancing them off each other. This is not an outrageously difficult task. In AstroDatabank we call this feature AstroSignatures. You can see how it works by going to www.astrodatabank.com/ASEveryAstrologerAResearcher.htm..

Summary

I would like to lay to rest the notion that astrology is essentially incompatible with scientific research. All the scientific research that has been done thus far is too simple to get any impressive results. Doing research on how many journalists are Geminis is a ludicrously simple research design. And yet the failure of such research is trotted out both by the hard-core scientists and hard-core mystical astrologers as proof that astrology cannot be subjected to scientific investigation. We are on the cusp of an era when we can prove them both wrong. We'll not only prove astrology works but also improve astrology by being able to put our techniques to the test and find out which ones are highly reliable and which are only used to confirm more powerful factors.

No matter how sophisticated quantitative techniques get, there will always be a place for qualitative astrological research. Qualitative research produces the richest and most useful results for the consulting astrologer. I would like to see lots more research done on astrological syndromes and the highest and lowest expressions of the astrological archetypes. Articles like the one Glenn Perry wrote for The Mountain Astrologer on the Leo-Aquarius axis, Dana Gerhardt's series on fairy tales and the Zodiac, and Donna Cunningham's articles on the highest and lowest expressions of different aspects with the outer planets. We need more information on the lowest and highest expressions with lots of examples from real lives.

The great artists all did studies in between their great works to hone their techniques. Reading more books is not going to improve your craft as a master astrologer as much as doing systematic studies of real data. Thanks to Lois Rodden we have lots of pre-categorized data that we can access by biographical trait or astrological factors. I invite you to test some of your favorite little aphorisms against the data of famous people and clients that you import into the database.

Simple exercises like pulling up all the people with Pluto conjoining their Moon and looking to see how the expression changes in each house will teach you new things.

One of the biggest challenges in doing readings is to find ways to communicate to clients the potential in their chart. It would be great to have more data-based books on astrological syndromes and what has been done with them. Examples would help communicate to clients ways that they can step into their greatness. Professional astrologers are the ones who are best qualified to write the articles that give us the stories and examples to pass on to clients.

I wish you fun and fruitful research.

* * * * *

Mark McDonough is the president of AstroDatabank Company. AstroDatabank develops and publishes Lois Rodden's AstroDatabank software program - the largest collection of accurate birth data for learning and research. AstroDatabank.com publishes charts of people in the news with commentaries from serious astrologers. AstroDatabank Company also publishes AstrologySoftwareShop.com - the most comprehensive guide to professional-grade astrology software on the web.

USING THE INTERNET TO EXPAND YOUR PRACTICE

by Rick Levine

When you decided to become a professional astrologer, you knew that you would have to learn basic skills like horoscope calculation, chart delineation and a basic repertoire of astrological techniques. You probably also realized that basic computer skills were necessary for operating the chart calculation software of your choice. But you may not have realized that Internet skills would also be important while building your practice. In fact, the Internet offers the self-employed astrologer a way to hang out a shingle that is visible all over the world.

The first thing you probably need to decide is what kind of astrology you will be doing. What you do on the Internet will be determined by the types of client interaction you seek. Will you be doing phone consultations or will you only be seeing clients in person in your office? If you are not interested in doing phone consultations, then it really doesn't pay for you to use the Internet to advertise your services to someone in another city, state or country. But for those of you who are comfortable doing phone work, your potential clientele is greatly increased by removing the geographical constraints of local advertising.

You must realize that the Internet is not the get-rich-quick scheme that some thought it was in the mid-90s when it was characterized as the world's "first zero-billion dollar" industry. Many people became certain that there was easy money to be made, but not many were successful at generating profits. Nevertheless, the Internet is growing, e-commerce is expanding, and even though there continues to be a shakeout in the dot-com market, the Internet is not going away.

As a new medium, the Internet is a rapidly changing environment. What is written today will be outdated by the time it is printed. In 1998, John Warnock, the founder of Adobe Systems said, "Everything we know to be true about the Internet will be proven wrong over the next five years." An Internet strategy devised just a year ago may now be hopelessly out of date. Playing the Internet game can be quite exciting, but it does take a hands-on approach to be highly successful. There are, thankfully, many different levels on which to engage the Internet. I will outline some of them here, along with some specific tips to maximize your efforts.

The Internet has changed the way we do business. It connects people like no other medium, and we astrologers can capitalize on this. The Internet is very personal inasmuch as each one of us will use it differently. Rather than creating a list of "shoulds," I strongly encourage each astrologer to create your own relationship with the Internet and find a way in which to incorporate it into your business practices. What works for one astrologer will not work for everyone.

Perhaps the most attractive thing about the Internet is the thought that we can make our services available to millions of potential customers. By creating even the simplest of web sites, we can give people access to our marketing material 24 hours a day, seven days a week, twelve months a year. Even if you are unknown, the Internet can level the playing field between you and more established astrologers. If this all sounds good…it is! But it is not as simple as "if you build it, they will come." There are millions of web sites out there. A simple search on the word "astrology" returns nearly 2 million pages! It is rather overwhelming! How would someone find your needle of a site in that haystack of pages?

Earlier, I said that the Internet connects people. It is this feature that you must always keep in mind. You must always be thinking about how you can connect to others and how others can connect to you. Connections make the Internet work. If you are isolated on the Net, then you are not really "on the Net."

So, where to begin?

Obviously, if you haven't already, the first thing you need to do is get a computer and get connected to the net. How to do that is outside the scope of this chapter, but I would like to make mention here that there are many different ways to be connected to the Internet, and *how* you are connected can be important. Most people are connected via a "dial-up" account. This means that when you want to be on the Internet, you instruct your computer to use a modem that dials a number through your regular old telephone line. Needless to say, this is better than no connection at all, but it has three drawbacks. First, it is slow. Second, it ties up a phone line. And third, you must go through the dial-up procedure every time you want to do something on the Internet. There are two common alternatives, both of which are considered "broadband" access. Broadband access is not available everywhere. You should find out which services are available in your area. The first type of broadband access is DSL. The second is a cable modem. DSL uses your regular phone line. A cable modem uses your cable TV line. Neither of them gets in the way of your regular services, so you can be talking on the phone while using your DSL connection or you can be watching cable TV while using your cable modem. Broadband connection is many times faster than the fastest 56k telephone modem. And, with broadband, you are *always on the Internet.* This can make a big difference in how you use the Internet.

Once you are connected to the Internet, the next question is what do you do now? You will need an ISP, an Internet Service Provider. The largest ISP is America OnLine. Many people choose AOL because it is easy and ubiquitous. In fact, these may be the only two reasons to use AOL. In some geographical regions, AOL is desirable because there are local access numbers if you have a dial-up account. I'm not going to bash AOL, because it does serve a purpose, but you will never realize the full potential of the Internet while accessing it through AOL. Even if you are only using the Internet for email, AOL is limiting. Whether you are on a Macintosh or using Windows, there is good email software that gives you much more power and ease of use than trying to keep up with email using AOL. Do a bit of research and find a reliable ISP in your locale that meets your needs. Most ISPs will include a web site with your email account. Creating a website is an important part of using the Internet to expand your astrology practice.

Before we get into the issues around creating your own web site, let me go on record stating that using email may be the most important Internet skill you can develop. Whether or not you plan to create a web site for yourself, you can make use of the Internet by using email. Remember, the Internet is about making connections. Since so many people have email these days, I recommend that you get an email address for every client you see. As part of your client intake, record birth data, mailing address, telephone numbers AND a valid email. I enter each client into my Outlook contact file. Your email list can become one of your greatest assets. It is a relatively simple task to create a monthly newsletter and email it to everyone on your list. There is no postage cost, delivery is nearly instantaneous, and it is a great way to keep your name in front of clients and potential clients. Make sure you get your client's permission to send them your newsletters and with every email newsletter you send, include instructions to be removed from your emailing list. This is very important. You never want to send an email to someone who doesn't want it. This is more than just bad karma; it's bad netiquette (net etiquette). Many ISPs will not tolerate it.

So, what can you write in your client newsletter? Let your imagination be your guide. Many astrologers use their email lists to write about current planetary configurations.

Some astrologers write about a current event, a celebrity, or their predictions. Whatever you choose to write, remember to be concise. Email works best when you get to the point. Also, in your email newsletter, include short notices about your services, classes you are teaching or upcoming lectures. This is your way to stay in touch with your clients. In fact, your goal is to foster a feeling of community amongst your clients. If they feel a part of your group, chances are they will return to you when they need another reading or recommend you to others. Make it easy for them to contact you.

Email takes time. If you distribute an email newsletter, expect your subscribers to email you back with questions and comments. It may seem obvious, but *answer your email!* You don't have to write a book in response to a question, but at least let the person know you've received their email. Try to give a short reply. If someone emails you their birthdate and a specific astrological question that you cannot answer without creating a chart and plying your trade, don't be afraid to tell them that you receive many emails and that you cannot do their question justice in the time you have available for email correspondence. Let them know that you are available on a fee-for-time basis and that is how you make your living. There is nothing shameful in that kind of response. On the other hand, if I can help someone with some good information in a few minutes, I will do that for free. It comes back many fold. Remember, your daily email time is like working the crowd at a trade show. This is a form of self-promotion, but if you are too pushy you will offend folks, and they may not want to continue to receive your emails.

While we are on the subject of email, there are many email lists that you can subscribe to. An email list is sometimes called a discussion group. You can subscribe to a particular list by sending an email to a particular email address. There is no cost for subscribing to email lists. Once you are subscribed, you will receive emails sent to the special email address used by the list. If you send an email to the list address, *everyone* on the list receives your email. If *anyone* on the list sends an email, you and everyone else receives it. This creates an ongoing chat about a variety of topics, but rather than "real time," it is all done via email. There are astrological email lists on just about every topic you can think of. From general topics to Vedic, horary, psychological, medical, celebrities and technical. Not only can you learn some good astrology on these lists, but you can also get your name out. Let people get to know you from your participation. Remember, the Internet is about making connections.

Of course, when most people think about using the Internet to expand their practice, they think about making a home page or a more intricate web site. Here is where it can get sticky. The most important lesson is don't bite off more than you can chew. On the very simplest end, you can create a "brochureware" site. This is a single web page or several pages that are like your brochure. They are static; that is, they don't change. You build them once and they remain on the web. It's like having a billboard. A web site must have a URL, a Universal Resource Locator. A URL is your World-Wide Web address. You can use the URL given to you by your ISP such as http://www.your-isp.com/yourname/index.html. Or you can register your own domain name. Most ISPs will charge a minimum amount to register a domain for you. A domain name costs about $50 per year, and you may pay your ISP $20 per month or more to maintain your address. Your domain name will give you an URL like www.yourname.com. Domain names like astrology.com, astronet.com, astrodatabank.com, mooncircles.com, stariq.com and uacastrology.org have been registered by individuals or companies. Your ISP can help you check to see if your name or your company name is still available.

Once you have a URL, you must then create your web pages or hire someone to make them for you. This is not much different than creating a brochure. You will need to write the text and come up with a graphic look and feel. Additionally, you'll need to decide what topics you want to have available and how to allow your site visitors to navigate through your pages.

Aside from having some brochure type pages, there are other kinds of content you might want to consider. If you are the writer type, think about adding a new article or column once a week or once a month. If you are sending out an email newsletter, send it out with an announcement about each new article you have available on your site. You can include live links that will take your email readers directly to your site. Your goal here is to drive traffic to your site. Once people are on your site, they can be gently reminded about you and your services. Remember, although the Internet may be fun for some people, we are specifically addressing using it to expand our astrology businesses. Make certain that your navigation allows your site visitors to access information about your services and/or to contact you via email from every page on your site.

Here are some tips to keep in mind as you build your web site:

Always think about ways to create virtual community. You could even start a mailing list of your own. Service like Yahoo Groups make it inexpensive (free) and easy.

Integrate, don't isolate. Always look for ways to make connections. Find related sites on the Net and send them an email introducing yourself and your services. Look for ways to work together. For example, offer to give a weekly or monthly column (perhaps the same one you write in your email newsletter?) to a site for free in exchange for a prominent advertisement or link back to your homepage.

Involve your clients and visitors. Invite them to register for your free email newsletter. Get them to participate.

Change content. A static brochureware site becomes stale. A client will visit it once, come back a second time and see no change. If, on the third visit there is still no change, chances are he won't be back a fourth time. New content brings users back for more.

Spend time on the net. Know what's out there. See what other astrologers are doing. Link out to them. On the Internet there is more business than you can handle. Don't be afraid of sending someone (via a link) to another site. If it's a good site, they will be back to your site for more.

Most importantly: think outside of the box. Be adventurous. Be innovative. The Internet rewards quick thinking and clever action. Use guerilla-marketing techniques. You don't need a lot of money. You just need to think like the Americans during the Revolutionary War. You are fighting for your life as an astrologer. Be bold.

Work the net. Get your site listed in search engines. There are several excellent sites that give tips for getting your URL into the major search engines. There are free and fee-based products that will automatically register your site with search engines. Create a link banner and then exchange link banners with other sites. The more places on the net there are for people to find you, the more people will actually come to your web site.

Participate in online directory listings. Many sites offer astrologers and other practitioners a place to list their services, fees and contact information. The Metalog director is a fee-based service. Complete information on this directory is available online at http://www.astrologer.com/intro.html. The Astrologer's Directory on StarIQ is a free service with information about participation available at http://www.stariq.com/Main/Astro-Directory.htm.

Integrate print media. Publish your URL and your email address on your business cards. If you have a printed brochure, make certain your web address and email address are prominently displayed.

How much should this all cost? The cost of launching and operating a web site can run into the hundreds of thousands, even millions of dollars per year. Programming, graphics, copywriting and administration expenses all can add up. On the other end of the spectrum, you can create your own homepage and have it hosted by an ISP for a few hundred dollars. It depends how much you decide to do yourself. There are many programs, like Microsoft FrontPage that let you build your own homepage without having to learn HTML, the computer language that is used to create web pages. There may be some pain in the initial learning, but it can be well worth it to be able to be the captain of your own web ship and to be able to create your own web pages.

The Internet is vast and complex. It certainly can be overwhelming. As you launch your astrology business or as you expand your existing business, you can use the Net to make contact with many more people than previously possible. Regardless of your Internet goals, one thing is certain. The Internet can help you grow your business, even if you only take baby steps at first. In the beginning, it can be frustrating as you learn your way around, but there is great potential. If you are uncertain, find yourself a friend who is Net-savvy and develop that relationship. Although you may want to hire someone to create your web site (assuming you don't want to do it yourself), it is a good idea to have a friend with whom you can think through your Internet strategies and use as a reality check when needed. Even if you are technophobic, you must realize that the Internet is here to stay, just as radio, television and computers. You don't have to become an Internet geek. You don't need to learn programming languages to make use of the Net. You just need to embrace the new technology as you would any tool. At minimum, use email. To get more involved, get yourself a web site. Or, roll up your sleeves, prepare for some late nights, and jump into the cyberpool and start swimming.

* * * * *

Rick Levine is a practicing astrologer and an active voice in the community. He is President of StarIQ.com, which serves 40,000 subscribers with personalized transits via email. He is Past President of the Washington State Astrology Association, and a member of ISAR, AFAN, NCGR and OPA. He was a Founding Trustee of Kepler College.

TEACHING ASTROLOGY & BECOMING A SELF-PUBLISHED ASTROLOGICAL AUTHOR

by Robert P. Blaschke

Excerpted from Robert's forthcoming book:
Astrology: A Language of Life
Volume III - A Handbook for the Practicing Astrologer
Earthwalk School of Astrology Publishing
0-9668978-2-X * March 2002

Opening Perspective

During my third Jupiter return at the age of 35, I resigned from my career as an Architectural Hardware Consultant in San Francisco to live my dream of being a full-time professional astrologer. I walked away from a $60,000-a-year financial package which included my salary, a company car, paid gasoline, auto insurance, health insurance, life insurance and a retirement account.

When I followed my heart in 1989 to do what I loved full-time, knowing that being a part-time astrologer could never get me to the depth of astrological knowledge that only full-time immersion would bring, my progressed Midheaven was conjunct my natal eleventh house South Node, my progressed Ascendant was conjunct my natal second house Neptune, and my progressed Mars had just ingressed into his dignity in Scorpio, joining my four natal planets there. Anyone other than an astrologer would have said, "What was he thinking?" Believe me, I have posed that question to myself many times over the last twelve years when I looked in my checkbook and saw only single or double digit numbers in the balance column.

I have recently reached my fourth Jupiter return at the age of 47, and I have found myself reflecting on the growth and expansion that has come into my life over these last dozen years. I succeeded at my goal to make it as a full-time astrologer, author and lecturer, and I have several hundred regular, loyal and satisfied clients all over the U.S., Canada and abroad. I founded a school of astrology, I built an astrological mail-order business, I became an astrological software dealer, and I started an astrological publishing company and have written two books with a third on the way.

Now, I feel that I can share my experiences to help other astrologers either just starting out, or trying to make the leap from a part-time to a full-time practice. The intention of my third volume in the Astrology: A Language of Life series is to produce a practical handbook for the self-employed astrologer that addresses all of their concerns regarding transitioning from student, establishing a professional practice, handling income, expenses and taxes, marketing and advertising, lecturing and teaching, participating in the astrological community, navigating the client relationship, writing and publishing, overcoming occupational hazards, and fostering personal/spiritual growth. This article is excerpted from Chapters Five and Eight in my new book, "Lecturing & Teaching" (5) and "Writing & Publishing" (8), and it is my hope that it will make a pragmatic contribution to this work.

Teaching Astrology

My experience has shown me that when you are building an astrological practice, teaching beginning astrology classes is the engine that pulls the entire income train down the tracks. Beginning students become regular clients, buy astrology software, books, tapes, charts and reports from you, refer family and friends to your practice, go on to take intermediate and advanced classes, attend your lectures and workshops, and remain a part of your loyal customer base for years.

I have taught beginning astrology classes at community colleges, metaphysical centers, local Theosophical Society chapters, new thought churches, several different bookstores, and at my school here in Portland, Oregon. I have taught classes with as few as three students, and with as many as twenty-five to forty at community colleges and Theosophical Society chapters. Recently, I was invited to join the faculty of the ONLINE College of Astrology, an Internet astrology school with AOL-style chat rooms (classrooms) where the students and instructor meet weekly for question and answer sessions; with homework, reading assignments and chart analysis projects in between classes.

The astrologer with a newly established practice finds out in a hurry how erratic clientele income can be. The wear and tear on the astrologer's nervous system from his concerns over fluctuating monthly income may affect the functioning of his intuition during consultations. As I wrote in Chapter Four on "Marketing and Advertising," yellow page ads and display ads in alternative magazines or practitioner directories can never accomplish what referrals will. The repetition required for any ad to produce consistent new customer contact can take as long as three years. For referrals to occur, the astrologer has to take himself to the potential customer base, rather than wait for the clients to come to him through advertising – get out and teach!

Wherever you live, there are teaching opportunities for the resourceful astrologer. You can approach your local bookstores, community college continuing education departments, metaphysical centers, psychic institutes, new thought churches, coffee houses, new age gift stores or any other venue that you feel would have an interest in offering a class.

You will need to design a course outline, and I recommend that the beginning class be no longer than eight weeks. The following is the beginning course I have taught for years: Week 1: Elements, Modes & Zodiac Signs; Week 2: Planets; Week 3: Houses; Week 4: Aspects I; Week 5: Aspects II; Week 6: Planetary Patterns & Aspect Configurations; Week 7: Chart Synthesis; Week 8: Student Chart Examples. You are welcome to e-mail me at ewastro@rain.com and I will send you my detailed class syllabus for your reference. The textbook I use for my beginning class is Chart Interpretation Handbook by Stephen Arroyo.

To receive a 40% discount off of the book cover price (you pay shipping), and thus be able to make a small profit selling textbooks to your students at retail, you can call CRCS Publications in Sebastopol, California at 707.829.0735 (the publisher of Mr. Arroyo's books) and set up a wholesale account for yourself as a school of astrology. If you intend to teach regularly, it would be wise to bring in a few other titles from CRCS written by Mr. Arroyo, Bil Tierney, Tracy Marks or Liz Greene and create a small bookstore in your classroom. Don't forget to charge and report state sales tax for books, but tax is not required for student tuition payments.

About 3 to 4 of every ten beginning students will want to go on to your intermediate class. I recommend the following eight-week course outline for your next level of instruction: Week 1: Retrograde Planets; Week 2: Transits; Week 3: Progressions; Week 4: Lunar Nodes & Life Purpose; Week 5: Relationship Analysis Techniques; Week 6: Aspects & 360š Cycle Analysis; Week 7: Solar Returns; Week 8: House Rulerships & Dispositors.

Your intermediate class should only be scheduled every other quarter, thus allowing the completed beginning students to accumulate and ensure better registration for this class. I would recommend teaching the beginning class year-round, offering it four quarters a year. The Fall quarter should end before Thanksgiving, and the Winter quarter should begin after New Year to avoid conflict with the Holidays.

I have charged from $95 to $300 for my classes, depending on length (6, 8 or 12 weeks) and whether I was paid the tuition directly, or if a percentage was kept by the facility where I was teaching. I feel that a $15 per class tuition basis is fair, thus an eight-week class with a compensation to the astrologer of $120 is par for the course in most cities in the U.S. and Canada. If you are teaching through a bookstore, where they keep a percentage, you will have to increase the tuition in order to net this amount for yourself. I have generally charged $35 for my local monthly or twice-monthly Saturday workshops, which were usually scheduled from 11:00 AM to 4:00 PM.

My income as an astrologer from teaching locally at my school and at other venues here in Portland, where I have taught over 300 students, reached as high as $3900 in class tuition during 1993, and $2650 in workshop tuition during 1998 and 1999. This combined tuition income represented about 1/6 to 1/8 of my overall gross income. The resulting income in other areas of my astrology business, i.e. consultations, software sales, books, tapes, reports, etc., derived from these students is hard to estimate, but was a significant contribution to my gross income each year.

Now that I am in a different stage in my career as an astrologer, where I receive, as an author, speaking invitations to lecture and teach throughout the U.S. and Canada, my income is earned from different sources than when I was building my practice. What I valued most about the local teaching were the stimulating intellectual relationships I developed with my students, and the confidence I gained to evolve into a national lecturer.

How to Become a Self-published Author

When I started researching and writing my first book on Progressions in 1997-98, I was faced with a big decision. Would I submit my manuscript to an established astrological publishing house, hope for acceptance, work with an editor and a marketing department, and pray that the book would retain its core meaning and value? Also, being a Scorpio, I did some clandestine investigation into royalty payments, debits from returned inventory by distributors and retail booksellers, and what other author's experiences were working with a publisher. What I heard and discovered was not a pretty picture, financially and otherwise, so it took me about three impulsive risk-taking seconds to say to myself, "Go for it!"

I have Mars rising, Jupiter conjunct the MC, nine planets Eastern and Sun trine Uranus, not to mention a second house Neptune, so I realize that I am more independent than the average astrologer and more prone to believe that financial visions can come true. For any of us who step into astrological self-employment to pursue our dreams, risk-taking and autonomy are virtues, and I hope that my efforts will inspire other astrologers to take the plunge. My publishing company is my retirement plan. I have a vision of writing seven astrology books, and I believe that the cash flow from these book sales, along with the lecturing income that has accompanied my becoming an author, will sustain me in my golden years. It is also my dream to create an author's guild when my publishing company stabilizes financially, allowing me to publish other astrologers through a shared-expense program.

Starting my publishing company was actually quite simple. To design my first book while I was writing my manuscript, I simply took C.E.O. Carter's *The Principles of Astrology* off my bookshelf, and scrutinized the table of contents, page layout, cover design and title pages. Using my 1993 Macintosh PowerBook with Microsoft Works version 3,

I created a page template for a 5.5" by 8.5" book size with 0.5" margins left and right, and 0.4" margins top and bottom. This was accomplished by choosing horizontal orientation in page setup, and the manuscript text would then cover half an 8.5 x 11 page. I had a detailed chapter outline that I wrote from, and to foster a healthy sense of psychological progress as I went along, I would "build" the book page by page, printing each page as I wrote it, folding and cutting the 8.5 x 11 in half with a letter opener to represent the finished 5.5 x 8.5 page.

Little by little, my book became a stack of single-sided laser printed half sheets on my desk, and holding it in my hands as it grew in size provided a lot of forward momentum for me. I started to think about my book project as if it were a construction job as in my previous career. There was a scheduled completion date (Jupiter's direct station of November 13, 1998), and all the subcontractors were required by contract to complete their work by that date, or incur steep penalties from the general contractor such as withheld payment, liens, etc. I pictured myself as the general contractor (publisher), and all of my multiple personalities as the subcontractors (writer, researcher, cover designer, marketing director, etc.).

You will need to include a title page(s), a table of contents with chapter topic and page number references, and any appendices or planetary tables should follow the main manuscript. A bibliography can go at the very end, as can your manuscript footnotes. Printing quantities and press run dates can go on the title page. I have also included appendices for my catalogue of lecture, class and workshop tapes, computer chart services, software programs for sale, and contact information for me to be invited to lecture, consult and teach.

An astrological author must have an editor. No matter how fine a Virgo ascendant you may have, or how exacting a Venus-Saturn conjunction in Scorpio one may possess, there is no substitute for a trained second pair of eyes to go over your manuscript. At this point in my progress, I received a miracle from an angel. One of my former students, a writer and an editor, agreed to work with me. Patricia Laferriere has made me a better writer by her superb editing of my first two books. I gave her the nickname "Chainsaw" when I first got my edited manuscript back. My long rambling paragraphs were cut into two or three smaller and more concise ones. Patty's stamp on my writing was acknowledged in the following book review of Progressions:

> "Blaschke is an excellent teaching writer. He knows exactly how to introduce his material in small, precisely measured increments, cite his authorities with clarity and brevity, and guide the reader through virtually frustration free assimilation and mastery of progression theory and application. After reading this book and working within the guidelines presented, many of us might begin to wonder why we had not learned these techniques sooner. The answer is that there probably weren't enough teachers or writers of this man's caliber available when we first began the study and practice of astrology." - Joan Star, Geocosmic Magazine

To visualize publishing my book, I made a list of what I would need to acquire and accomplish before my scheduled completion date: a) an International Standard Book Number (ISBN); b) a Library of Congress Catalogue Card Number; c) a scannable bar code for the back cover, d) a retail price; e) cover art; f) back cover photo; g) back cover content synopsis; h) someone to write a foreword for me; i) a software program capable of sophisticated page layouts in order to build a front and back cover plus the book spine into one document; j) quotations from three different printers; k) a financing plan to pay the printer; l) distributors to sell my book to retail booksellers; m) an Advantage Account program with Amazon.com to market my book on the Internet; n) a display ad in The Mountain Astrologer magazine to market the book directly to astrologers; and o) a data base of book reviewers who write for various astrology publications to whom to send review copies of the book.

To create your publishing company, you will need to acquire an "ISBN Log Book" (International Standard Book Number), which is an initial set of ten ISBN's that you assign to each of your titles. These ISBN numbers are issued to identify the publisher, and for distributors and retailers to place orders and maintain inventory control, and are the central hub of the existing system for book identification worldwide. They can be obtained through the United States Agent, R.R. Bowker Company in New Providence, New Jersey toll-free at 1.877.310.7333. You will then receive your ISBN Log Book, along with an "Advance Book Information" form that you will fill out and return to R.R. Bowker for your first title. A sample ISBN looks like this: 0-9668978-0-3. The Canadian Agent for ISBN numbers is the National Library of Canada in Ottawa, Ontario at 819.994.6872.

If you do not have a name for your publishing company, you will have to create a business entity for it. In Oregon, this simply means registering the company name with the Secretary of State's Corporation Division Business Registry Office for a small filing fee. In California, for example, you would have to file your company name with the Office of the County Clerk, and then place a "Fictitious Business Name Statement" in a local newspaper for four issues. I simply took my existing company name, Earthwalk School of Astrology, and used it as the name of my new publishing company.

Once you have established your publishing company, and then add titles as each new book is written, you simply go on-line to www.bowkerlink.com and update your title information in their "Books in Print" section. As a publisher, you are responsible for updating this data base as each new title is published.

Before you publish your book, you must submit a "Request for Preassignment of Library of Congress Catalog Card Number" form to:

Library of Congress
Cataloging in Publication Division
101 Independence Ave. SE
Washington, DC 20540

This government agency can be reached at 202.707.6372 and has an automated phone system through which you can listen to general information and request these forms. This number is used to classify book content within the nation's library system, and is not mandatory to have for publishing a title, but recommended. Once you establish your publishing company, and then add titles as each new book is written, you can simply go on-line to www.pcn.loc.gov/pcn and fill out the preassigned card number form on-line.

No distributor will accept your book into their system unless it has a bar code on the bottom right hand corner of the back cover. This bar code must also contain the ISBN number, along with the cover price and a country code. R.R. Bowker has a list of all "Bar Code Film Master Suppliers" in the United States, and this list can be obtained by calling them at 1.877.310.7333. Your printer may also be able to provide the bar code to you during the cover proof phase of your printing job. I got my bar codes from a company in Carmel, California called "Publisher's Resources" at 1.800.528.3535. They can e-mail you or your printer the bar code as an attached EPS or TIFF file.

Next, you will have to determine a retail cover price for your book. This is a very important decision with hidden and drastic financial consequences if done carelessly. Book distributor's contractual terms are brutal: they get a 55% discount off of the cover price, then resell your book to the retail bookseller at a 40% discount, thus making a net 15% profit in the process. They exist on a volume sales basis, and you will not see a dime from them for 90 days after their sale to the retailer, and then you are only paid for the single monthly sales which occurred four months ago. You, as the publisher, will also have to absorb "damage and defective" returns, as well as paying the freight coming and going. As you can see, cash flow is a huge problem for a new small publishing company.

You have to set your cover price high enough to absorb this discount to the wholesale distributor, and you have to print enough copies to get a low enough unit cost per book from the printer. My Volume I on Progressions has a cover price of $14.95 and Volume II on Sabian Aspect Orbs sells for $18.95. I based my pricing decision on three factors: a) page count; b) the printer's quotation for three different press run quantities; and c) my perception of maximum fair retail cost per book.

Deciding on cover art for your book will take you into a very creative area of self-publishing. I chose to have an artist paint an oil painting of the Sabian Symbol for my lunar degree, 7 Pisces, as my first book cover. My second book cover is a pastel pencil drawing of the Sabian Symbol for my solar degree, 23 Scorpio. Volume III's cover is a drawing of the Sabian Symbol for my Ascendant, 22 Virgo. The original works of art are then scanned and saved as TIFF files for importation into your cover design software program. My second book also contains several black and white illustrations, done by the same artist who did the cover, and these were also scanned and saved as PICT files and then imported into Microsoft Works as each chapter's frontispiece.

You will also need to have a back cover photo taken. I recommend having a friend take this picture rather than a professional photographer. You will save money for one thing, you will be more relaxed and natural, and you won't be persuaded to assume one of those mawkish studio poses with your head cocked to an affected angle with your chin resting foolishly on the palm of your hand. This photo, whether color or black and white, can then be scanned and saved as a TIFF file.

The back cover will require more than your photo, the bar code and the retail price. You will also need to come up with a synopsis of the book's content, your biography as the author, and include excerpts from your foreword. I use bulleted text from my table of contents to serve as my back cover synopsis. The upper left hand corner of the back cover should contain "Astrology," and the upper right hand corner should contain the retail price. Your publishing company's name and address should appear in the bottom left hand corner, with the bar code placed at the lower right.

It is customary and traditional to ask another astrological author to read your manuscript and write a foreword to your book. Note carefully how this word is spelled. The most common error in self-published books is the misspelling of this word as forward. I consider myself very fortunate to have had Robert Hand agree to write the foreword for Progressions, and Lynda Hill to write the foreword for Sabian Aspect Orbs. You can approach an author at a conference, or call them directly and ask them if you may send them your manuscript. You should initiate this contact at least four months prior to your desired publication date, as author's schedules are often quite busy, and it will take some time for them to get to your project.

Now comes the do-it-yourself graphic design phase of becoming a publisher: using your page layout software to design your book cover. I have used QuarkXPress version 3.32 for the Macintosh to create my book covers. First, you need to estimate your final page count and call a printer and have them calculate your book spine thickness. For example, my second book was 258 pages, and my printer advised me that the spine would be 9/16" (.5625) thick. Then, go into your software program and create a new document with horizontal orientation. For a 5.5" x 8.5" book, the cover needs to be trimmed to a 8.5" x 11.5625" final size. Make two text boxes of 5.625" x 8.625" size on either side, and put a spine text box of 0.5625" x 8.625" in the center. The reason that the text boxes are slightly larger than the trim size is called a bleed, where any element that touches the trimmed edge of the page must be made to extend beyond the edge of the page at least .125" (1/8").

Starting with your front cover, which will be the right text box, make a rectangular picture box in the center which is mathematically proportional to your original artwork, leaving a top margin of about 2", and a bottom margin of about 1.25". Import the TIFF file of your artwork scan into your picture box. Then, create two text boxes top and bottom. Place your book title (and subtitle) in the top box, and your name as author in the lower text box. You can also place the name of your illustrator or foreword writer beneath your name in a smaller font size. Choose a color for the background and a color and style for your font. Make sure you choose "None" for your background color in the two text boxes.

For your back cover, which will be the left text box, you will need to create six smaller text boxes and two picture boxes within it. The two picture boxes will contain your photo and bar code. The text boxes (with "None" selected for your background color) will contain your subject category (Astrology), retail price, foreword excerpts, biography, content synopsis and publisher name and address. You are welcome to e-mail me at ewastro@rain.com, and I will send you an attached Quark file of my book cover layout.

Finally, rotate your spine text box to -90š, and put your last name at the top, the book title (subtitle) in the center, and your publishing company name at the bottom. Congratulations! you have now designed your book cover.

Next, you will want to get quotations from at least three different printers to compare prices competitively. You have three options for printing your book. You can offset print both the text and cover, you can offset print the cover and digitally high speed print the text, or you can digitally high speed print both the text and cover. New printing technology, such as the Xerox DocuTech 6180 machine, can print your book just like a high speed laser printer. The Xerox DocuColor 40 machine can digitally print your cover just like a color laser printer. You can supply your printer with "Print Ready Electronic Files" of your manuscript and cover, sent via e-mail as EPS (encapsulated PostScript•) attached files. The only difference in quality between the two printing options is that the digitally printed books will have a slight ripple in the pages, viewed from the edge, similar to a page run through a laser printer with the heat required to dry the toner.

A printing of 500 books will be less expensive using digital high speed printing for both the text and cover. For 1000 books, offset printing will be slightly less expensive. For 1500 books or more, offset printing will be significantly less expensive. To give you an idea of my printing costs, Progressions, a 152-page book, cost me $6350 for a 2000 copy second printing which was offset printed, about $3.17 cost per book. Selling this $14.95 book to the distributor with a 55% discount means that I am paid $6.73 per book, a gross profit of $3.56 each. Sabian Aspect Orbs, a 258-page book, cost me $3640 for a 500 copy second printing which was digitally high speed printed, about $7.28 cost per book. Selling this $18.95 book to the distributor with a 55% discount means that I am paid about $8.53 per book, a gross profit of $1.25 each. Now you can see why I don't mind flying around the country lecturing to different local astrology groups, carrying boxes of books with me to sell at the full cover price. It is the only time that my publishing company makes any money!

I recommend the following two printers:

Eugene Print, Inc.
1000 Conger Street
Eugene, OR 97402
800.688.4741

Thomson-Shore, Inc.
7300 West Joy Road
Dexter, MI 48130
734.426.3939

You can shop locally for a third printer from whom to get an additional quotation. I recommend the following specifications for your quotation on a trade paperback book:

your page count (including title pages and appendices)
text = 60# white
cover = 10 point, C1S (coated one side); 4 color process
binding = perfect binding in 32's
trim size = 5.5 x 8.5

You can save printing costs by going to a 2 color cover, but you will diminish the aesthetic quality of your book. I realize that with my Mars in Libra, this is an important consideration for me as a publisher. If cost is your primary concern, you could shave several hundred dollars from your printing quotation by doing this.

Unless you have a few thousand dollars in your savings account, or room on your credit card limit, publishing your first book will require some creative financing. Your printer will have you fill out a credit application, but most likely you will have to pay for the first printing when you go to pick up your books, or before they are shipped to you. I placed an ad in The Mountain Astrologer magazine, in the same issue as my book excerpt article, offering a pre-publication discount on Progressions to raise money to pay the printer. This was a smart move for me, as within the first three weeks after the magazine came out, I received over 125 advance orders from eleven different countries, resulting in over $2000 of pre-publication book sales. I was able to pay the printer when I picked up my first printing of 500 copies without going into debt, pulling the rest of the invoice amount from the cash flow of my practice and school. Since then, I have been on open account status with them, and have 30 days to pay the invoice after I pick up the books.

To market your book beyond direct sales to astrologers, using display ads in astrology magazines, you will need to enter into consignment contracts with book distributors. They will order a full case of books from you (about 35 to 70 depending on how your printer packs them) on consignment, store them in their warehouse, and ship them to retail booksellers as they receive orders from the bookstores.

The contract terms require you to give the distributor a 55% discount off the cover price, you pay the shipping, and you will not be paid until 90 days after the end of the month in which sales were made. The check will sometimes be held an additional 30 days after that. Damaged or defective books will be returned to you as the publisher, with the book cost and shipping deducted from your payment. There are two major consignment distributors for astrology books in the United States:

BOOKPEOPLE   New Leaf Distributing Co.
7900 Edgewater Drive   401 Thornton Road
Oakland, CA 94621   Lithia Springs, GA 30122
510.632.4700   770.948.7845

BOOKPEOPLE ships mostly to bookstores west of the Rockies, and New Leaf covers East of the Rockies. You can contact the small press buyer at each company and request a contract be sent to you. They will require a review copy of your book to ensure that it has a bar code, ISBN, proper binding, etc. before they establish your consignment account and send you your first purchase order.

Amazon.com has an Advantage program for small presses and self-published authors. You can establish your account on-line at www.amazon.com/advantage. They will also require a 55% discount off the cover price, and you pay the shipping to their warehouse in Lexington, Kentucky. You will have to send them a sample book for a cover scan, and they will then build a web page for your book, and also link it to the title name and author name in their site search engine. When I am not lecturing to local astrology groups, this is where I sell most of my books.

Customers will write reviews of your book, rank it in a five-star system, and you, as publisher, can have book review excerpts posted on the web page. They pay you 30 days after the end of the month in which sales were made, and you never see an invoice or purchase order. Everything is handled through e-mail, except for your check arriving in the mail. I ship my books via USPS Media Mail or Bound Printed Matter (book rate).

Amazon.co.uk in England will also carry your book in their on-line catalogue. You can reach them via e-mail at listing-titles@amazon.co.uk, and they will send you instructions on how to proceed. However, they do not purchase books through either BOOKPEOPLE or New Leaf, so you will have to establish another distribution account with either Ingram Book Co. in La Vergne, Tennessee (615.793.5000), or Baker & Taylor in Charlotte, North Carolina (1.800.775.1800). You can call either of these distributors and ask to speak to a small press buyer and they will send you a contract application package in the mail. These two companies are not consignment distributors, they will issue actual purchase orders for specific quantities of your titles, and the terms are net 90 days for payment with you paying the freight as usual. It is worth the extra effort to have your book available overseas, and Amazon also has websites in Germany, France and Japan that buy from these distributors.

When your book is published, you will want to send review copies to astrology book reviewers around the world. My books have been reviewed in The Mountain Astrologer, American Astrology, Dell Horoscope, Geocosmic, AA Journal (UK), AFI Journal (New Zealand), FAA Journal (Australia), NCGR memberletter, The International Astrologer, Considerations, The Wholistic Astrologer, Aquarius Workshops, Welcome to Planet Earth, Data News and other publications. Book reviews are far and away the best marketing vehicle for a publisher. One good review in a respected magazine or journal by a well-known reviewer can result in sales of hundreds of books.

One other positive manifestation of being an author is the development of literary relationships with book reviewers around the world. These individuals are highly intelligent, well-read astrologically, and fine astrologers themselves. It is a pure joy to read a review of your book by an individual who fully grasps your theory and technique. You are welcome to e-mail me at ewastro@rain.com and I will send you my data base of book reviewers around the world that I have worked with.

Conclusion

It is my sincere wish that the systematic information contained in this article will help you to earn additional money as a professional astrologer by teaching classes locally. It is also my hope that any of you who have the aspiration to write and self-publish your first book will find pragmatic help in this article to take you one step closer to your goals. I am available for professional consultation to discuss any of your concerns in getting your publishing company off the ground. We all can learn from each other's triumphs and failures, and mine are always an open book to my fellow professional astrologers. Namasté. © 2001 Robert P Blaschke

* * * * *

Robert P. Blaschke, owner of Earthwalk School of Astrology in Portland, Oregon, is a full-time professional teaching and consulting astrologer. A third house Scorpio Sun with an exact trine to Uranus, and a Pisces Moon with Virgo rising, Robert has had a life-long passion for astrology, beginning his studies in 1971. He is a past-president of both the Oregon Astrological Association and Washington State Astrological Association, and past National Coordinator of the ISAR Professional Astrology Speakers Bureau. He has lectured at regional, national and international astrology conferences in the U.S. and Canada, and has been a requested speaker for many local astrological associations. For years he has taught classes and workshops at community colleges, various bookstores and metaphysical centers, and at his astrology school. His articles have appeared in The Mountain Astrologer, KOSMOS, Geocosmic, NCGR memberletter, The Journal of AstroPsychology, The Ascendant, Astraea Astrology, Réalta and other publications. He is the author of the highly acclaimed Astrology: A Language of Life series; Volume I - Progressions and Volume II - Sabian Aspect Orbs.
Robert P. Blaschke, Astrologer, Earthwalk School of Astrology
PO Box 19778
Portland OR 97280 USA
503.246.8250
Author: Astrology: A Language of Life
Volume I - Progressions (ISBN 0-9668978-0-3)
Volume II - Sabian Aspect Orbs (ISBN 0-9668978-1-1)
Volume III - A Handbook for the Practicing Astrologer (March 2002)
mailto:ewastro@rain.com
http://www.amazon.com/exec/obidos/ts/book-glance/0966897803
http://www.amazon.com/exec/obidos/ts/book-glance/0966897811

PROFESSIONAL SPEAKING

by Carole Devine

Whether you plan to make speaking to groups a small part of your professional practice or a mainstay, you will want to be as professional as possible in order to garner the rewards such opportunities provide you. It isn't enough just to know your subject; you should also have some general information about the nuts and bolts of the speaking profession. There are many places to speak where you can hone your skills until you become comfortable, and at the same time it gives you an opportunity to meet your community and to foster more understanding of our profession which is generally misunderstood.

Obviously, if you are going to speak on astrology, you need to have the credentials to do so and should have some kind of certification to validate it, but if you feel awkward about your speaking skills, then *Toastmasters International* is the place for you. When I joined, I had no idea how effective it would be. In a short time, because of the gentle critiquing of other members and the efficient way they zeroed in on what needed improvement, I had lost the "uhs and ahs" that are so distracting to audiences, had learned to pace myself and time speeches better, and had gained other tips too numerous to mention. It is the kind of organization you can stay in for life and continue to hone and perfect your skills.

The National Speakers Association is an incredible group of people. I never did join the national group, itself, but I did join the state chapter, *The Virginia Speakers Association*. In all my life, I've never had the pleasure of getting to know such a wonderful, generous and even spiritual group of people, although the word, spiritual, was probably never mentioned. I got to know members of the national group because so many of them gave weekends of their time to come to Norfolk and give us seminars on a regular basis. For about five years, I went to almost all of them. There are many things about the business of speaking that are important for astrologers to know and use.

First, if you are going to make speaking a mainstay of your income and practice, you need to have marketing tools. If you are going after high-paying, truly professional speaking opportunities, you will need a video of a portion of one of your talks, about 10 minutes, and maybe an agent, although it isn't absolutely necessary. However, if you get an agent, s/he expects you to keep your fees at the same level for all engagements, and expects a commission of some kind even on talks that are spinoffs from those you get as a result of an agent's referral. I chose not to have an agent because I wanted to work with astrological groups who are not able to pay the kind of fees agents expect.

One of the advantages of being in a organization like *The Virginia Speakers Association* is that they provide specially-priced services such as hiring a person to come to the group and video tape short presentations for the members' demo video. The person they hired also provided a wealth of information about how to make the best demo video possible. Just watching the process was an education in itself.

If you do not want to make speaking your main activity but still want to actively solicit speaking engagements, then an audio tape of excerpts from previous speeches is a must. For many, many years I foolishly taped nothing because I saw it at the time as being egotistical. I now wish I'd taped everything. You should tape anything at all you do in public because you will need something as a sample if a group has never heard of you. You can copy sections from several lectures to demonstrate your range of topics, combine them on one tape and send them out to organizations' meeting planners along with your bio, tear sheets or copies of articles you've had published, a copy of any books you have written, a detailed description of your lecture and workshop topics, fee schedule, "one sheet" (which I'll explain next) and a cover letter. I purchased cassette wells with adhesive on the back so that I could adhere one to the inner pocket of a two-pocket folder. These folders have slits for your business card on the left pocket, which I use for that purpose, but on the right pocket front there is space that is just right for a cassette-holding well.

The "one sheet" is a professional speaker's mainstay. It is a one page summary about you as a speaker. On the one sheet should be a good photograph, professionally done and screened by a printer for maximum reproductive quality, a biographical synopsis, endorsement quotes, short descriptions of your main speeches, and contact information. If you have an agent, the contact information should be his or hers, but if not, then yours. One sheets are best done on high quality heavy paper and in one or two colors if possible. They can be sent or faxed quickly to anyone asking for information about you, and then you can follow that up by sending your folder with demo tape, etc.

Once you have a speaking engagement, there are a few preliminary things to do. First there should be a contract of some sort spelling out the terms of the commitment, including the amount and when you will get paid and what expenses are covered. This should be very clear. The best and most satisfying speaking engagement I ever had was in St. Petersburg, FL with an astrological group that not only had a contract ready for me, but also had their own one sheet-type of synopsis about potential speakers on file with specific information designed for their own use. Very efficient! Be prepared. If a group does not offer a contract, have one of your own ready to send to them. Not only does it avoid any possibility of misunderstandings, but it also makes you look highly professional and someone to be taken seriously. In the contract be sure to mention discounts you will give the group on books, if you have any to sell, so they can make a commission on them. I give a 40% discount which is what a bookstore would get. This provides extra funds for the group, and they will appreciate it.

Ask about your audience ahead of time regarding range of age, professional bent, cultural background, etc. so you can tailor your presentation to them. After all, I've spoken to women's professional organizations, Civitan, Parents Without Partners, realtors and many, many other mainstream groups. Each will have a special set of circumstances around which you can tailor your talk. Ask about the room: what size, how it will be arranged, and what audio/visual aids and equipment are available for your use. I always take my own recording equipment just in case, and also carry around a flip chart and stand in the trunk of my car. If you can, it's a good idea to visit the meeting room beforehand so you can see if there will be outside distractions such as construction noise, air traffic noise, or even large crowds. Sometimes things cannot be avoided. Once there was a noisy wedding reception going on behind a folding partition that really made it hard to be heard. If your talk will be in a hotel with partitions like these, ask what will be adjacent to you. If it would be a potential distraction, *maybe* it can be changed. But don't be difficult. An attitude of non co-operation is deadly.

Prepare an evaluation sheet to hand out to your audience when you are finished so that you can possibly build or add to a newsletter mailing or email list, get an idea of where you need improvement in your presentations, and offer other services that your audience might find of interest. Have a place on this sheet for them to check if they'd like you to contact them for anything such as other lectures, classes, receiving a newsletter, having a home party, etc. How do you get them to give it back to you right then? Use the evaluation papers, after they have been filled out and handed back, for a drawing for door prizes which you provide. You can give away copies of books you've written, copies of tapes of other lectures you've done, or if you're speaking to a non-astrological group, it can be a free chart, or other item you think would be welcome. The idea is to get feedback and to give something to them so your name will not be forgotten. It is an honor to be asked to share your information with people, and generous of them to take time to listen to you. Give them the best you have.

* * * * *

Carole Devine, C.A., NCGR, has been a full time professional Astrologer since the mid-seventies. She is the author of Solar Arc Directions: How to Read Life's Roadmap, Celestial Gardening, and the 94-cassette correspondence course, Exploring Astrology. She has authored several columns in Virginia Beach, VA, Ft. Myers, FL and in The Mountain Astrologer. She has lectured to groups of all kinds for many years including Edgar Cayce groups in Europe about the Cayce Astrological material.

GROWING YOUR BUSINESS BY SELLING REPORTS

by Mark McDonough

Computerized Reports - They're Better than You Think

Millions of people read their horoscope in the paper each day, but only a tiny fraction ever experience an in-person reading of their whole chart. How can we build a bridge from newspaper astrology to your front door? Making an appointment for a chart reading is a big commitment of time, money, and identity. Most people don't have their chart done "for entertainment purposes only." To go through the effort of finding an astrologer, driving to the appointment, listening attentively for an hour and a half, and then paying a fee equal to several hours of one's labor, one must believe that astrology is useful. If "real" astrology is to become more popular, we need to offer readings whose cost and customization falls somewhere between newspaper astrology and a full in-person reading. Computer-produced readings are that middle ground, and those astrologers who offer computerized reports will have a second source of income and a much wider base of referrals.

But can a self-respecting professional astrologer actually sell computerized reports? Aren't they just cheesy hack jobs with zero intelligence? Well, they all used to be, and some still are. We know that computers can't possibly integrate as many factors into a report as we do when we examine the sign, house, aspects to each planet, and how the planets fit into bigger patterns that all tell a story. But computerized reports are better ambassadors for real astrology than you might first suspect.

81

I recently took on a project to review all the major report writers. I came to the project with a skeptical attitude. I had read too many unimpressive computerized reports, consisting of boring, confusing lists of one-paragraph descriptions for each planet's sign, house and aspects. However, I was pleasantly surprised by the current batch of professional-grade report writers. The writing is much fresher, more precise and more integrated than I recalled. I was actually stunned by the accuracy of the reports. I ran off samples for friends and read them the descriptions of their tight-orbed, hard aspects and they were also stunned. Some serious work has gone into re-writing these delineations that are now detailed and quite helpful.

These professional-level reports are not "for entertainment purposes only." They are serious attempts to give useful astrological information to people who are ready to get beyond Sun sign astrology but cannot afford it or are still too embarrassed to see an astrologer in person. They are a valuable bridge to an in-person reading. As a professional astrologer, you can use these reports as sales agents to increase your business. They are the appetizer that creates the hunger for more information.

Reports as Sales Agents for New Business

Each printed report goes out with your name, phone number and an explanation of the benefits of an in-person reading. With today's report writers, you can count on several paragraphs in the report to stun the reader with their accuracy. In some ways computerized reports are even more impressive than an in-person session. You know that astrology works when your core personal dilemma is laid bare by a computer that can't possibly be picking up any clues from your style of speech or dress.

Of course, computerized reports may miss big themes composed of multiple   planets, and clients often get confused with their contradictory interpretations. This is why they will come to see you to learn more. Your cover letter tells them that the computer is limited in its ability to present an integrated report. It promises that when they come to see you, the contradictions and amazing hits will all be wrapped up into a coherent, integrated story. They will learn things about themselves that they have sensed but were never quite able to articulate. They will feel seen in a profound way.

Not everyone is ready for the personal intensity of an in-person reading. The computerized report can be the bridge for them. It brings real astrology to more people. Many of the people to whom you sell reports will come back   for more. Some may tuck a report away for years and call you later. Many will show the report to their friends and you'll get some of their friends for clients.

Reports Create More Repeat Business

A great many reports are given free to clients and this makes good economic sense. It is much easier to keep a client than find a new one. The more you can do to enhance your client's experience, the more likely they will come back to you for another reading.

Reports help clients retain what you said in the reading. Just the act of reading something on paper helps people to remember better. Also, reading the same message from a different point of view often provides the "something extra" to make it click. Though reports are limited in their ability to integrate the pieces into a coherent picture, they are able to go into more detail than one can cover in a single session. The reports can be easily personalized by highlighting the tightest orbs or scrawling a few notes in the margin. Most reports let you edit them in your word processor before you print them so you can delete the less relevant paragraphs or add a few sentences of your own. Many even give you easy access to the delineation text so if you don't like their version of Moon-Neptune you can permanently change it to yours. The net result is that you'll be more helpful to your clients because they will retain more of your perspective and advice by taking home something written.

The reading will feel more substantial to the client when they leave your office with something in their hand. Clients usually find it more convenient to review written material than to listen again to the session tape. No one has the time to write out a full report, but it doesn't take long to annotate one.

Clients often take reports to work to show friends. Those friends may become clients themselves after hearing your client describe how powerful it was to have an in-person reading with you.

Compatibility and Forecast Reports

Clients who come in for a natal reading may wish to purchase a compatibility or forecast report before leaving. Many people have no idea how useful a synastry reading can be. It is very reassuring to see one's relationship issues written out on paper. It is such a relief to see that the difficulties are somewhat fated by the stars and that the relationship can be made much more satisfying with insight and compassion. It is a tremendous service to be able to give clients objective feedback on how they enter relationships, and on the particular dynamics of their relationship with their spouse, boyfriend, parent, child or sibling. The more information one has on what each person brings to the relationship, and the more insight one has on how each person's needs and expectations interact, the greater the chance of relationship success.

Like natal reports, compatibility reports can overwhelm clients with the amount of detail that they provide. Again, you can help overcome this by writing a few notes in the margins and using a highlighter to point out the inter-aspects with the tightest orbs. In some cases, the compatibility report is just a quick check on a new relationship. If the relationship is serious and long-lasting, many people will want to come back for a more in-depth understanding of the issues presented in the report. They'll want you to supply the full story behind all the details in the report.

Providing or selling clients a forecast report allows you to give the natal chart all the focus it deserves and still provide your clients with a complete service. Forecast reports are so much better than what your clients are accustomed to reading in the newspaper. Modern forecast reports do a much better job than their predecessors of pulling out the big transits and writing more expansively on their meaning and possibility.

Forecast reports keep astrology alive every day. A six-month report reminds your clients that it is time to order another report or book another appointment

I have long thought it a tragedy that there are so many single-session readings. There is so much more that we can tell clients about themselves, their relationships, and the meaning of their current struggles. Reports introduce clients to other areas of astrological expertise and to some of the details that we don't have time to go into in one session, but could if clients are willing to go deeper.

How Much Money Can One Make Selling Reports?

Natal reports generally sell for $15-25; compatibility reports go for $20-25; and forecast reports for $25-65. In absolute dollars it isn't going to buy you a new car, but it is a second source of income. Charging $15 - $60 for five minutes work is high-profit activity.

85

An astrologer from a small town in northern California told me that she made $50 -200 per week selling reports mainly to her existing clients. She also gives reports away to clients who come in on their birthdays or after the birth of a new baby. With Moon in Cancer she develops long-standing nurturing relationships with clients. Sometimes a client will call needing an immediate appointment and she's booked solid for weeks. In these cases the client often buys a compatibility or forecast report to hold them over until they can see her personally. They feel better and she does too.

People also buy reports as presents for others. Child reports are popular new baby gifts and a compatibility report may be given as a wedding or engagement gift. For the person who has everything, a forecast report is different every year.

You can sell reports at fairs, over the phone, or from your web site. They can be printed and mailed or emailed to customers around the world. If you have a web site and buy a report developed by Cosmic Patterns, they will set up a special page for you on their web site to sell these reports. They do all the credit card processing all you have to do is provide a link from your web site and you get 40% of whatever they sell from your referrals.

Selling reports makes money in two ways – you get extra cash for the reports, but most of all it helps build repeat business for in-person readings.

Which Reports Are the Best?

Which reports are the best? That is a very interesting question, and the answer is too detailed to capture in a short article. At the risk of sounding self-serving, the best place to go to get a comprehensive report on   all the major report writers is AstrologySoftwareShop.com. We have devoted many pages to comparative reviews of the major astrological report writers. We describe each report writer's writing style and its level of detail. We also provide the full text of each report using the chart of Robin Williams. To make it easier to compare writing styles, we have even pulled out delineations for the same chart factors from each report to put them on the same page. There is no other place to find this level of report comparison.

Each of the major charting software companies makes several reports that use the same file format as their charting program. What this means is that if you have already entered the data to construct a chart for someone, it is just a matter of a few more keystrokes to print out a report. Entering the birth data will take you more time then it takes to send several reports to the printer.

Computerized Reports Will Grow the Market for In-Person Reports

I built AstrologySoftwareShop.com to help fund further development of AstroDatabank, but in the process I became devoted to spreading the word about what computerized reports can do to further the growth of astrology. I believe that they have a valuable role to play in bridging the gap between newspaper astrology and full in-person readings. They are an inexpensive way for people to get an introduction into what real astrology can do for them. They also increase your repeat business by providing more value to your   client. They are good for astrology and also good for building your business.

* * * * *

Mark McDonough is the president of AstroDatabank Company. AstroDatabank develops and publishes Lois Rodden's AstroDatabank software program - the largest collection of accurate birth data for learning and research. AstroDatabank.com publishes charts of people in the news with commentaries from serious astrologers. AstroDatabank Company also publishes

87

FINANCIAL PLANNING IS FOR EVERYONE

by Michael Munkasey

The two distinct parts to financial planning are planning for retirement and investing. Each involve their own unique complexity and depth. Please realize that while these parts are related, even intertwined in many ways, they remain quite separate. Let us examine financial planning in particular so as to give you a better understanding of this element. Investment planning is another complex area, best handled on an individual basis.

There are several fundamental human drives like love, survival, the need for water and food, the need for recognition, the need to acquire and use possessions (or money), the need for human interaction, and so forth. Each person is unique in the way that they apply their own personality to the application and pursuit of these traits. One person may emphasize the need for communication but downplay the need for self (or other) love. Another person may place love as their highest priority while neglecting the need for acquiring property. Astrology is a discipline which allows measurement of each person's thrust in such areas. It is through the understanding of one's needs in such areas that a distinct financial plan can be established for each person. We each have our unique needs and thrusts in life, and these change often as life progresses, requiring an on-going reassessment of future pathways. That is what makes each life so unique and precious.

Why should one plan for their financial future? So that they can live comfortably after a certain age without having to rely on continuing to work for a salary to meet their basic living needs. The sad part of life in America today is that so few people, perhaps less than 30%, make and adhere to personalized financial plans. They may rely solely on government program largess to provide such future stability -- only to realize that when they reach retirement, the income from these programs barely takes them out of, or even keeps them in, the poverty level. Primarily this is due to the inflation of prices which has been fairly steady over centuries.

An effect of this inflation is that a person grows up seeing that housing or rent requires XX dollars a month, food is YY dollars, utilities are ZZ dollars, etc., and retains the mindset that it is these figures: XX, YY, and ZZ that will be adequate some future years hence. Or, a person relies solely on one pension plan, only to find some many years in the future that this pension, coupled with government programs like Social Security, only provides a monthly income at the poverty level. The effects of inflation can be so insidious that they remain unnoticeable, yet they remain.

Inflation does not need to be there, but the economic theory generally followed today promotes a creeping inflation as one means to increase our standard of living. This has other effects: it attracts people from other places to our country for the opportunities and jobs which this economic theory creates. It also devalues savings denoted in monetary terms, while inflating savings values of real property, like housing, oil wells, etc. In the far past these considerations were moot. A person could go into the "wilds" and hunt game. They could grow their own vegetables and grains. Nuts were on neighboring trees for the taking. But as the vast majority of people chose to live in communities which then grew into towns or cities, and take on specialized jobs -- as opposed to being generalists -- the opportunity to "walk into the forest and pluck fruit for breakfast" diminished, and they had to rely on a salary to purchase the fruit (or whatever) from a grocer.

Only one hundred and thirty years ago as the vast open lands in the central and western parts of the United States were being settled, the people moving in there had to do everything for themselves. They had to erect their house, tend their gardens, tend livestock and grow feed both for themselves and for cash sale, tend the chickens for eggs, cook, wash, increase their family (children gave them free labor), and on and on. These people had to be generalists. If the wagon's wheel fractured, they had to repair it. If the barn caught fire and burned, they had to rebuild it. If the local creek overflowed, they had to dam it. If they wanted lumber they may have had to travel many miles to chop suitable trees down and then haul the logs back to their house. If they wanted ham for breakfast they slaughtered a pig. Today, much of that life has changed. We have become specialists. If the local dam overflows and floods the bathroom we call a plumber. If we need eggs we go to the grocery, or a local restaurant which then prepares the meal for us.

The purpose of financial planning is to help a person reach their intended level of existence throughout whatever their life span may be. But financial planning is useless without accompanying good health -- and health is primarily associated with family genetics, mindset, and the avoidance of accidents. Those are outside of the scope of this article. Planning for one's financial future remains our focus. The first part of developing a financial plan depends on one and only one factor: your age. How old are you right now? People at ages twenty, forty, or fifty-five each need totally different financial approaches. The earlier in life one sets and then follows a financial plan, the easier it becomes to achieve this plan. A person may rely on promises of retirement at 80% of salary in thirty years. This sounds good. But, what if that retirement salary, thirty years hence, only places one at the then currently defined poverty level. In the 1950s in the United States the poverty level was defined as having to live with a monthly income of about $600. In the 1990s this figure had risen to about $2500. a month. More recently it has risen to about $3000. a month. Hence, a person retaining their 1950s mindset of only needing even a doubling of their $600 a month, would in the 1990s, find themself needing to continue to work for a salary in their retirement years.

Financial planning involves the following overall considerations, as a minimum:

- Determining one's age of retirement,
- Determining the level of living at that retirement, and
- Setting a plan to assure income to maintain that level.

Here is one example. I am thirty-five years old and I want to retire at age fifty-five with a monthly income of XX dollars a month. The current value of my savings and investments is YY dollars. I will assume that at retirement age I can earn GG interest per month on my accumulations. Therefore, in twenty years I need to accumulate ZZ more dollars in my retirement account. Here is my plan for doing that. Etc.

Let us see what needs to be done to achieve a viable financial plan. How old are you now? At what age do you plan to retire? What monthly income level do you expect then to maintain your lifestyle? What are you going to do now, today, to ensure that you achieve that level of income -- and then some? Will you rely on the stock market to increase your portfolio? Will you rely on your employer's pension? Perhaps coupled with government benefits like Social Security, Medicare, etc.? I don't think that there is any doubt that the best personal plan is one that does not rely on any of these. It is a personalized plan that provides an income stream adequate to maintain your desired level of existence, which can then be supplemented by an employer's pension, government programs, etc. What would happen, and this has happened with regularity, if the employer backing the pension plan you are relying on declares bankruptcy? Or is acquired or merged into a company which has a totally different (and more meager) retirement plan outlook? Do you really naively think that the acquiring company will generously continue to fund a more employee-lucrative plan into the distant future? Think again. This rarely happens.

Your individual retirement plan, which should be the cornerstone of your financial future, this independent single stream of future income, needs to be started now! Today. You begin to achieve your individual financial plan by saving a part of your income and placing or investing that wisely. The truthful dictum is "Pay yourself first!". Your initial payment to self or investment may be in a house and land. It may also include assets such as stocks, bonds or bank accounts which provide consistent income streams. The investment may be in gold, diamonds, oil wells -- whatever it is, it HAS to be there and working for your plan to remain viable. It can not remain thinking like I will save XX dollars this month, but next month I need YY to buy WW so I will skip my savings that month. That inconsistent thinking and action will not achieve your level of comfort years hence. Nor can you accumulate funds over several years and then decide to spend these on an immediate necessity. There is NO immediate necessity so great that it should impact your future income stream. Unfortunately, many people lack vision (Jupiter) and persistence (Saturn) in following their plans.

Here then is what you need to consider as part of your plan:

- Your individual plan (the most important option)
- An employer (or maybe more than one employer's) plan
- Social Security (the least reliable option)
- Investing
- Estate planning
- Health care

In general, Venus is money coming in and Mars is money going out. Also, Venus represents savings, and Mars represents the management of those savings. Today in the U.S. there are many wonderful plans, such as IRAs, SEPs, 401ks, Keogh plans, etc., that a person can take advantage of. Primarily these plans offer certain tax advantages which need to be assessed on an individual basis. There is the selection of such a plan (Venus), and then there is the management of such a plan (Mars). These forces need to work together. I do not wish to go into the specifics of each available option such as these plans. If nothing else, then having a personal savings account is mandatory. That savings account should contain enough balance to cover at least six months projected living expenses. What happens if a child needs extensive dental work? If the roof on your house starts to leak? If the transmission falls out of your car on the way to the grocery store? If your employer goes bankrupt? If a family needs expensive medical care, like a major operation -- and your medical plan only covers 70% of a $50,000 or more cost? Those funds are to cover shorter term emergencies like these.

People often make foolish choices with their moneys. Being involved in the financial planning arena I see this every day. A person receives a gift, a bequest, an inheritance or an annuity (it matters not what) and to them a large sum of money comes in. They are prudent and invest it wisely. Time passes, and that investment matures. All of a sudden more money than was originally left to them becomes available. But their new boyfriend or girlfriend or spouse sees a need for a new car, to pay off credit card debts, whatever - and poof!, those funds are gone. And when they are gone, they are gone forever. What represents years of accumulation and promise can be gone in a matter of minutes. It took years to accumulate, but minutes to spend. Rent? Spent!

A lecturer I heard recently defined expenses as anything which did not produce an income. Buy a new toaster, that is an expense. Buy some new clothes to keep up with fashion, that is an expense. And what do you do with your already overflowing closet? (A comic recently wagged: "How come my closet never has enough space in it if the universe keeps expanding?) Actions like those take money out of your possession. Putting money into stocks, bonds, a Certificate of Deposit (CD), rental housing, investing in a storage complex or a trailer park, etc.; those actions produce income. Thus, what are your priorities? After all it is your money! Is your priority income or expense? In which area do you place your largest concentration of effort?

Governmental plans such as Social Security or Medicare have their place. What is wrong about them is that they may provide a false sense of security. Social Security was never intended by the original planners to take the place of sound individual financial planning. It was meant to be used as a supplement to one's individual financial plan. Even at the top monthly bracket of Social Security payment, a person would hardly be out of the poverty level range. Do NOT rely solely on governmental programs such as these to meet your long term needs. They simply are not adequate for the needs of most people or families.

Taxes are another consideration when considering individual, employer, and governmental financial plans. Projecting on when to start such plans, planning on how to structure such plans, planning on when to implement such plans should each have an impact on your thinking. Taxes are inevitable, but they should not be considered to be an evil. Taxes pay for roads, schools, community management, defense (against invaders, floods, and many potential forms of destruction), the upholding of laws, the adjudgment of fairness in legal ways, etc. If you want to live in a society, then such benefits are helpful, even necessary. If you want a standard of living which gives you such protection, then you need to pay your fair share of taxes. You may object to your level of taxation, but you should not object to the inherent need for taxation. You may object to your particular tax circumstances as being unfair, but you need to consider the benefits you receive from living in your community. If you want the benefits of civilization and society, then you must honestly face payment for your fair share of upholding the infrastructure of that society. That means taxes.

Investing is an area of life which requires much attention. Few people have the time or inclination to follow investment paths. Everyone hears of investment opportunities, but how to take advantage of these opportunities, or how to assess the value of such opportunities, is an area of life for most people where they should consult experts. First off there are safety considerations -- how protected will my moneys be? (Saturn). Then there are return considerations -- what will I receive in return for placing my moneys here? (Jupiter). Then there is the inherent honesty (Mars) and fairness (Venus) of the people who are offering these opportunities. Centered on this are your individual needs (Sun) and domestic needs (Moon). Communication and thinking to structure these forces, to tie things together, to serve as "the middle man", is the domain of Mercury. Thus, in this area each of the visible planets has a distinct and unique role.

Estate planning includes planning for the passing of your estate (house, moneys, etc.) to those people or institutions which you select. Creating a will which states your intentions for such assets is mandatory. Not just needed, but mandatory. If you die without a will, then the state, or some strangers, get to decide how your estate gets divided up and to whom it should go. You may have worked eighty or ninety years to accumulate assets, but without a will, then at your death strangers get to distribute those. A will is mandatory -- I am repeating that. If you do not have a will today, right now, then today, right now, go out and get one filed. Do not wait. This is essential. This is not something to put off. Just "Do it!".

But estate planning involves more than having a will. Estate planning is more than carrying a life insurance policy. There are complex tax consequences which need to be considered in estate planning. Certainly estate planning depends on the size of the estate. But a couple with children who live in a house worth XX dollars, and maybe own a retirement acre or two in the woods, and have savings, and investments, etc. -- they need an overall and comprehensive estate plan. They need to appoint an Executor of this plan. They need to consider the granting of Powers of Attorney should they become incapacitated. They need to direct what they wish to be done should they become incapacitated, or become mentally incompetent. They should consider their burial options -- as well as payment for same. Such planning is better done beforehand, and officially registered, than at the time of a crisis.

Last but not least, your financial plan would be deficient if it did not include planning for health care and coverage for health emergencies. This area again, like all of these areas, is complex and involves many options, each of which are best considered on an individual basis. Planning for long-term care for yourself, or a parent, or a close relative is an important part of financial planning. Do you have a contingency plan for long term care for yourself? For a parent or relative? Do you carry adequate insurance for such? Or, will you simply rely on governmental or local health care charities to take care of your problems? This is a complex area, but is one which can not be ignored.

In summary, you should now better understand the need for making an adequate financial plan, and the overall complexity of such a plan. Generally, most people are not capable of creating and drafting their own financial plan. There are insurance agents who will create a financial plan for you at no cost, but only if you also purchase insurance policies through them. The advantage of this, of course, is no cost. The disadvantage is that the centerpiece of such a plan will be their insurance policy. I hope that through this article I have convinced you that financial planning involves much more than purchasing one or a series of insurance policies. Also I am not addressing the cost built in to that insurance policy for such "free" planning. It also makes little sense to have an insurance agent come out and create a plan for you, and then refuse his or her policy and take the plan and work from there by yourself. That is short-range thinking and often becomes counter-productive. Don't do that.

Look for and identify a competent financial planning professional. Make an appointment to see this person. Professionals in this field often have certifications and letters denoting such certifications, like CFP (Certified Financial Planner), CLU (Chartered Life Underwriter), etc. Achievement of such credentialing involves a lot of time, effort, and expense on their part. Mostly these are certifications that are given by financial societies, as opposed to governmental sanctions. The SEC (the U.S. Securities and Exchange Commission) requires a series of examinations from certain financial planners, like their Series 65 license, which is for the "Registered Investment Advisor" or RIA. People who obtain such credentialing certainly meet prescribed educational guidelines and perhaps even levels of ethics. Thus choosing a person with such credentialing is probably better than taking advice from a co-worker, or a person you ride the bus with on your daily ride to work.

Work with the professional you select. Select the person based on their experience, knowledge and integrity -- not on what they charge you. Lawyers or accountants are not generally the best financial planners. Be cautious about selecting a lawyer or accountant recommended to you for financial planning purposes. If financial planning were their immediate thrust, then why would they employ financial planners to manage their estates? Provide the person you select with the information they need to create your overall plan. Work with that plan -- this is perhaps the most important part of what you need to do. Review that plan at least annually to ensure that it is meeting your needs. Go on to enjoy your retirement years. (C) 2001

* * * * *

Michael Munkasey has a BS in Mechanical Engineering from the United States Coast Guard Academy and an M. E. Ad. (Engineering Administration) from George Washington University. After spending many years in the Coast Guard, including service in the Vietnam theater, he worked as a Computer Information Scientist in the general scientific and medical communities, and for the public transportation (bus and subway) industry. Michael has been actively studying and practicing astrology since 1969. He holds Professional Astrologer's certifications from the American Federation of Astrologers (PMAFA), The Astrologer's Guild, and holds the Level IV certification from NCGR (NCGR - IV). NCGR is currently the world's largest organization devoted to the study of cosmic and human interactions. Michael served on the Board of NCGR from 1976 - 1996, and his last position was as "Clerk," their most important organizational position.

Michael has lectured internationally, presented papers at scientific symposiums, written hundreds of articles and letters, and appeared on many radio and television shows. Michael's books include: "The Astrological Thesaurus, Book 1, House Keywords," 1992; "Midpoints: Unleashing the Power of the Planets," and "The Concept Dictionary," both released in 1991. Michael is a recipient of many awards, including the Matrix "Pioneer of Astrology" award, and the Professional Astrologers, Inc., award for the most outstanding astrological lecture of 1992. Michael has also held state licenses which legally enable him to make personal and home loans; sell life, accident, disability and health insurance; sell annuities, give retirement advice, and recommend trades on the NASDAQ. Michael, a former ship's navigator, has a star in the constellation of Sextans (the sextant) named for him.

Michael is currently studying for the "Registered Investment Advisor" (RIA) certification from the SEC. Michael is the Senior Vice-President of "The Samuel Edwards Group" (TSEG). TSEG is a private club which offers a variety of financial opportunities to its members. As the club (soon to be) RIA Michael is involved with helping others plan their financial futures.

BUILDING AN ASTROLOGICAL COMMUNITY

by Ray Merriman

This title may sound a bit like an oxymoron. How do you build a community consisting of individuals who are astrologically ruled by Uranus, the planet of individualization and independence? It's not easy.

Furthermore, I am not so sure I am a person who could be considered an expert on this subject. Although I had the great privilege of presiding over ISAR through 6 years of fantastic growth and accomplishments between 1994-2000, it is also true that I left behind an organization that is not entirely at peace, or on good working terms, with its sister organizations. I was, in retrospect, a strong leader who kept the troops (directors and members) focused on their goals and vision, but alas a controversial one whose personality and motives are seen on completely different ends of the spectrum, depending upon who you ask.

But having gone through the experience of leading a very powerful, intelligent, and motivated board of directors consisting of leading world class astrologers, it would be impossible NOT to have learned something about building an astrological community. Even if I failed in some areas, I should have learned at least what DOESN'T work. And that can be just as useful as learning what DOES work.

What we achieved at ISAR between 1994-2000 was really quite remarkable, given the normally combative atmosphere between astrological leaders throughout our community. Our membership went from slightly over 200 members in the early 1990's, to close to 1000 at the present time. Our Treasury went from slightly over $30,000.00 to over $100,000.00. Many of our board of directors received the highest awards offered in astrology during this time for their outstanding contributions to field of astrology. And most importantly, we all shared a sense of love and respect for one another. We truly enjoyed working with one another, and we looked forward to those times when we could actually meet together, whether on a phone conference call, or in person at a conference. We did indeed create a strong, caring bond with one another, something akin to a family. And our relationship with our membership was also superb. Thus we had the sense of a community. Not only that, but we had a sense of a community that was growing in a healthy direction. The projects in which we were involved were perceived to be beneficial to astrologers everywhere. Everyone wanted to be a part of this energy, and we were proud to be the center of this vortex of growth. More than that, we were proud to be astrologers, and so were our members.

There are many reasons why we succeeded for quite a long time, whereas other groups appeared to struggle. It may have been just a matter of luck, or "good aspects." But it may also have been due to the fact that we consciously TRIED to build an astrological community, with a well-defined identity. In this regard, I can attempt to share with you what we did, or tried to do. I can share with you some of those things that I think contributed to building the sense of an astrological community, and hence a collective state of mind that kept us intact and strong.

Briefly, building a community, for ISAR, involved the following things: Developing a Common Vision, attracting a Compatible Working Core, moderating Respectful Dialogue and Exchange, encouraging Innovative Ideas, creating a Safe Environment where everyone feels that they are Contributing to the Manifestation of the Group Vision or Identity.

Common Vision:

Actually there is nothing common about developing a vision at all. It has to be an attractive and appealing vision that everyone shares. Everyone must "buy into it," so to speak. If you want to build a real community, it can't be the vision of just one individual. It has to be a vision that everyone feels a part of. And to do that, you have to take the time to hear everyone's vision. Everyone has to listen to everyone else express their hopes, their wishes, for the group. Then you begin to see where the different individual visions can connect with one other.

In fact, you don't necessarily see it all by yourself. Everyone begins to see it, or each person begins to see different aspects of their vision relating to someone else's vision. Before long, a synchronicity of realization begins to hit everyone at once. It is what this group of astrologers lived for. It was brainstorming leading to realization. It was pure and positive Uranian energy at work.

But it starts with vision. Someone has to share a vision with others. It has to have some appeal to those who are part of this discussion. The best way to get this process in motion is by leading a core group into focusing on the greater group that they represent. It can't be a personal vision. If you are going to build a community, it has to be a vision for the community. It has to be a vision that does one of two things: *It has to provide a perceived benefit for the members of this community, or it has to solve a problem that is present in this community*. And it has to be a benefit or a solution to a problem that everyone in the community recognizes. That is where it starts.

And then others in the core group - the board of directors, if you will - have to respond to it. They have to understand it and accept it. They have to agree to it. Or better yet, they have to add on to this vision, or modify it in some simple way, or share a completely different vision that answers one (or both) of the same two universal concerns just mentioned.

A transformational process then begins to take place in this central group. As they communicate their vision, or their understanding of the vision that someone else has presented, they begin to identify with it. They become a part of the creation of this group vision. The fact that their vision is transpersonal - *that it transcends the personal and focuses upon the good of the greater group* - instills trust and goodwill in the participants towards one another. They KNOW they are involved in something good. It is always harder to share a vision if there is the perception that someone stands to gain personally on an individual level from it. Either everyone in the community gains equally, or at least no one stands to gain more than anyone else does. It has to have this transpersonal, or humanistic quality to it, or else it runs the risk of splintering later on.

In the middle 1990's, I offered a simple challenge to the 9 members of the ISAR board, and 5 or 6 of its advisors. I simply asked them: "What would you like to see astrology become? What role would you like to see astrology assume on the world stage?" We all agreed that we wanted astrology to play a vital role on the world stage, and to do that, we believed that astrology and astrologers needed to advance as a credible profession - not just to the world at large, but to ourselves as a professional community. How could we help make that happen? How could we do it in a manner that our membership would support? And most importantly, we had to agree that doing this would either solve a major problem for the community, or would have enormous benefits to members of this community. When we listened to everyone's vision, it was a given that collectively, we could come up with something meaningful that would answer these questions.

Attract a Compatible Working Core

Once you define the vision, the next step was getting the right people together, and in the right roles, who could manifest that vision. In this regard, creating a *sense of harmony and good will* between all working players was essential.

The dynamics of people working together is extremely important. As in all relationships, *trust* is probably the most important factor. You have to have individuals who trust one another. You have to have a leader that the working core trusts, and vice-versa. The leader is the one who has to discern who can work together, and who can perform various roles most effectively. The leader has to ask him/herself many questions, such as: can this person do the job? Is this person reliable and responsible? Is this person's personality apt to get along well with others on the project? The leader may have to talk to the current members of the core to find these things out.

The first question here is also extremely important: can this person do the job? A project is only as strong as its weakest link. If everybody, except one person, does his or her job, then the job isn't done. Not only that, but one person out of synch with the rest of the group can cause frustration amongst the others. It can grow into a terrible distraction. In time, it can be a source of bitterness that begins to undermine the entire group. Thus it is important to find the right person, or people, for the right positions.

There is another reason why this is important. People will do their best if the job they take on is in an area where they have a passion. It is important for the group, and especially the leader of that group, to pay close attention to what others in the group are saying. This is most true during the vision process. It is here that individuals may express the areas of their passion. Try to identify those areas of each person's passion. Then give that person responsibility in that area - if he or she wants them. Not only that, but also see if there are other

105

people who share the same passion, and ask yourself: Can these people work together? Are their personalities compatible? If they share a passion for the same areas, and if their personalities are compatible, then the work will go much smoother. Things will get done, and the process will be enjoyable for each person.

The board of directors, or the central core of leaders for the community, also needs to share these attributes on a broader scale. As President of ISAR in 1994, I took great care to suggest candidates to the board of directors whom I felt could work well together. I took great care to study what roles needed to be filled, and who in the community might have a passion for doing this type of service, fulfilling that type of role. If I found someone who I thought could do the job, who had a passion for the role we needed, and who would get along well with the other members of the board, I would ask the board to consider this person for the next election, or as an appointment.

Moderating Respectful Dialogue and Exchange

It is OK to disagree with one another's proposal. What isn't OK is to give or take the disagreement personally.

Astrologers, like most people, are sensitive. They get attached easily to their ideas and long for approval and support for these ideas, especially in a group or community setting. There is a very thin line between constructive criticism and disapproval, depending on where you are sitting in the relationship. You may think you are offering constructive criticism. But the person who is the subject of your reply may be interpreting it as personal disapproval. That person may act defensively to your criticism, regardless of how well intentioned you tried to be. A conflict could flare up quickly, and suddenly there is tension in the core group. Before long, tension in the core group can evolve into a polarity within that group. Eventually people start choosing sides, and it filters down into the community. Instead of a community built on consensus, you now start building political parties. Instead of having respectful differences, you have groups that define their positions, and that of others, as "good and bad, " or "right and wrong."

But I digress. The leader of the group has to step in and guide the group discussion back to a respectful dialogue and exchange. He or she has to do this quickly, or the all-important trust between the members of the group becomes violated.

Moderating a discussion between intelligent people who make numerous proposals - not all of which are going to be accepted - is a fine art. It is difficult doing this in person, or even on a phone conference call. It is even more difficult trying to do this via email where the personal qualities of voice inflections cannot be heard. But this is where the importance of being an effective leader comes in. This is why groups with leaders who are skilled in this area tend to do so much better than groups which have no clearly defined leader. It is imperative for the leader not to let him/herself get personally bogged down in these potential conflicts.

Encouraging Innovative Ideas

There are two ways to guide a group, or a community, into a strong coalition. The first is to find a brilliant new idea that everyone finds appealing, positive, and exciting. Everyone wants to rally around a great new concept that has these qualities, especially if others they respect are excited about it. They will band together to create or build this thing they see as "good for the greater whole." The other way to build a strong coalition is to find (or create) a common enemy, or issue, that everyone hates. No one wants to be associated with a loser, or something that others agree is an evil, or negative. They will band together in the purpose of combating or destroying it.

Most (but not all) astrologers prefer the first option. Most astrologers subscribe to universal principles, metaphysical "laws." And one of these is that the power of creation is ultimately stronger than the power of destruction. As a matter of fact, the first usually leads to the second. When something positive is created, there is oftentimes an opposite reaction that tries to undermine or destroy it. But creation was first. It was original. Destruction and undermining are second. They are reactions to the creation itself. And *reaction* is fundamentally a weaker force than *creative action.*

A healthy astrology community – one that is built to last – must always subscribe to the first principle, the creative one. With ISAR, we aspired to this creative principal in regards to our board of directors and then to our membership. Before long, the entire board felt comfortable bringing up all kinds of exciting new proposals, without fear of rejection. The members of the core group would listen to these ideas, and discuss whether or not they were workable. In many instances, we would offer these ideas to our members for feedback. This in turn would generate more innovative ideas from our members. Everyone had the opportunity to share his or her voice. New and exciting ideas were encouraged and acknowledged. And oftentimes, these innovative ideas became the foundation for new projects, because we all understood what was appealing to the greater group (the community). We then took the structure of those innovative ideas and figured out ways to make them do-able.

Creating a Safe Environment for Contribution

First of all, you need to create a structure for exchange of ideas within the community. Originally this was done via our quarterly journal. However, that did not allow enough opportunity to exchange ideas between one another. Eventually we came upon the idea of a weekly ezine, where members could exchange ideas with one another every week. A moderator, Joyce Hoen, would review all material before it was printed, to make certain that it was respectful.

The important thing, however, is that members of the community needed to feel two things. First, they needed to feel that it was "safe" to share ideas. They needed to know that if they shared something as personal as an "idea," that it would be respected, that it would not be trashed and burned. By and large, most people do not enjoy combat or confrontation. They are not willing to risk embarrassment, humiliation, or degradation that oftentimes comes from rejection of their ideas.

Second, members of community must feel that they are part of the growth, or evolution, of that community. That is essential if they are to strongly identify with that community. For this reason, *there must be avenues developed that allow and encourage contribution, especially along the lines of the community vision*. It is not so important that individuals be encouraged to share ideas of a personal nature, or of a nature that enhances their personal standing only. That is akin to advertising, and has the effect of separating that person outside of the community. But what is important is to encourage members of the community to share ideas - especially innovative and appealing ones - which are of interest to the whole community. When a person does that, they are beginning to identify themselves as a vital part of that community. This must be encouraged in order to develop a strong and growing community. The more people who contribute dynamic ideas that benefit the community, or help solve a community problem, the more possible it becomes to manifest the community vision.

Special problems can arise when a member of the community or core group makes an innovative proposal that benefits the whole community on the one hand, but him or herself personally on the other hand. Or, perhaps that person offers a solution to a community problem, but that solution provides personal benefit or gain to him/herself. This can result in a "conflict of interest," and if not checked early, can lead to schisms within the community or core group. This can be a very difficult obstacle for the community to overcome. It is especially difficult when the person in the "conflict of interest" is a part of the core group, or board of directors. As leaders of the community, it is absolutely essential that each director maintain a community perspective in their behavior and decisions. They must put the needs of the community ahead of their own personal ambitions when acting in this role.

The concept of providing a safe environment, and thus encouraging members to contribute their innovative ideas and therefore identify strongly as a vital part of that community, brings up another important concept to successfully building a community. It is what I call a "Ground-Up" approach to management, as opposed to a "Top-Down" style. Leaders must be in touch with those who make up the grass roots of the community. They must not only encourage participation and sharing of ideas, but they must listen and respond respectfully to these ideas. Far too often we see communities splinter because the leaders - the core group - insist on making the rules and policies for the community. No one likes to be told what to do. Very few people enjoy a relationship that puts them in the "child" role of a parent-child pairing. Like children, members of a community are likely to rebel if their leaders act like parents. A safe environment that encourages respectful dialogue and innovative contributions *from everyone* fosters an adult-adult relationship between the leaders and the other members of the community. That helps to build a healthy community.

Conclusions

Building an astrological community is not an easy task, but the rewards for those who become involved in the process can be great. That is not a "conflict of interest," but a simple truth. When you decide to become active within any group that tries to create something positive, you cannot help but to benefit. The experience of working with motivated, like-minded people, transmits a confidence and enthusiasm that spills over into all other areas of your life. Even though you may be volunteering an enormous amount of time for this cause, you find your own personal career benefits as well. It may be because you are energized and empowered from working with such an exciting group. It may be due to the fact that others recognized the quality of your efforts, and word spreads about your good efforts. It is known as "tithing" in the religious community, and pro-bono in the professional community. Or it may be due to another universal principle that many astrologers accept: if you love what you do, and do what you love, the universe has a way of providing for you.

* * * * *

Raymond A. Merriman is the President of The Merriman Market Analyst, Inc. He is a financial markets analyst, and editor of the MMA Cycles Report, a market advisory newsletter that specializes in stocks, interest rates, currencies, precious metals, and grains. He served as President of ISAR, the International Society of Astrological Research from 1994-2000. He is a recipient of the Regulus Award for Enhancing the Image of Astrology as a Profession at the 1995 UAC conference. He is also the author of several books on Financial Astrology, including the series on The Ultimate Book on Stock Market Timing, Volumes 1, 2, and 3.

US VERSUS THEM: ASTROLOGY AND THE PROFESSIONAL WORLD

by Joanne Wickenburg

For years I believed that astrologers would never, at least in my lifetime, be accepted by the professional world. THEY would not allow it. I saw no means for astrologers to integrate astrology with other professions that would benefit greatly from it if they would only open their doors and permit astrology to enter. But THEY would never accept us. Even those using astrology in professional counseling who had Ph.D's in psychology would always need to keep a low profile with regard to their use of astrology in order to maintain respect within the professional community.

I was wrong.

Could it be that astrologers' greatest limitation is their own limited perceptions about what is possible for them to attain with regard to social acceptance? Have astrologers become so defensive that they have lost their objectivity? Interesting thought, isn't it? It certainly doesn't reflect the state of mind that we would expect from astrologers. We teach our students, and we tell our clients, that by understanding the "message of the stars" and aligning our lives with celestial cycles, all problems are surmountable. An understanding of the astrological chart empowers us all. But here we are, still considered piranhas by the professional world, unable to integrate with THEM or receive the respect we so covet.

Perhaps we haven't found the right aspect to empower us. We haven't found the right astrological configuration to allow this acceptance to occur. Perhaps when Pluto moves into Capricorn, society's rigid views will collapse. Or, perhaps it is US who have been closed-minded, and our limitations are largely self-induced. Have we been living in an illusion all of these years?

I wonder if our lack of recognition by the professionals in our world is founded on our own notion that we don't believe they will accept us? Maybe it's time for us to "reframe" the window we've been looking through for the last few hundred years. Maybe we need to take down the shutters that obscure our view and look at the larger landscape.

Do astrologers who want to be accepted by the professional world inadvertently separate themselves from it out of fear of being rejected? Or out of a belief system that says it simply can't happen? Or perhaps we are so attached to our own title, Astrologer, that we are unable to share the stage should we have an opportunity to integrate with other professions. The process of merging always requires change and letting go of some ego-attachments.

We often become defensive when our credibility or the merit of our highly valuable system of knowledge is questioned by the uninformed. Some of us try to prove our integrity by offering to read our skeptics' charts. Sometimes that works; more often it doesn't. Some of us respond to our critics by stating: "You have never studied astrology. How can you criticize something that you don't understand?" This is a fair argument, but is seldom productive in changing minds regarding astrology's value. At best, the argument is abruptly ended with an agreement that the critic does not understand it; therefore s/he will make no further comments regarding its authenticity. But that's where the conversation ends. No real progress has occurred.

Maybe we're using the wrong language when we are interacting with other professionals. Maybe the old "tried and true" defense for astrology is not the best approach. Maybe a new strategy in is order.

Since my involvement in the creation of Kepler College, I've gone through a change in my perception of THEM and have come to a new understanding about why astrologers are not welcome in the professional world. No, this short article is not a commercial for Kepler College, and I don't believe that acquiring an academic degree in astrological studies is the best route for all astrologers to travel. I do believe, however, that something very important can be learned as a result of the experiences that occurred throughout the process of the College's creation and from its interaction with THEM...the academic authorities. It certainly changed my perceptions.

On our first on-site visit with the Washington State Higher Education Coordinating Board (HEC Board), we were invited into a conference room. The director, the assistant director and a secretary sat with a two-inch stack of papers in front of them. They had printed Kepler's entire website! If memory serves me correctly, the first words exchanged were initiated by the assistant director. "What do you think you are doing?"

Was I intimidated? You bet I was!

Gary Lorentzen, a fellow Board member, had accompanied me to the meeting and was the first to respond. "We believe that it is time to bring to light the important role that astrology played in the development of civilization and to explore its relevance in today's world from an academic perspective." Gary cited some examples of the historical importance of astrology and members of the HEC Board began to show an interest. "History" was a word that they could understand. It didn't matter to them that Pluto was in Sagittarius and major changes in higher education were on the astrological agenda. We didn't talk about Pluto or Uranus; we talked about research, history, astronomy and so forth. A door opened to us because we were speaking to the members of the Education Board using a language with which they were familiar.

Only minutes into the meeting I witnessed a significant change in the body language of the HEC Board members and an open discussion regarding academic studies ensued. By the end of this meeting, the Board was giving us advice. We were stunned that we were not put in a position that required us to argue or fight for our rights. We entered the meeting prepared to fight, but instead, we were treated with respect once we demonstrated that we could speak in their language. We were merely challenged to demonstrate that the Kepler BA and MA degree programs met all academic requirements, incorporated all core competencies required by all college degree programs, and that certain policies and financial requirements were in place. We were prepared. We left the meeting with a sense that the HEC Board was supportive of what we were doing. The Board found the Kepler program interesting and recognized its academic integrity. Needless to say, we were shocked!

On the drive home from that historic meeting, I experienced an "epiphany". No longer did I feel we had to defend astrology's credibility. In our interaction with the Higher Education Board, there had been no need for warfare. I found it particularly curious that at no time were we asked if we "believed" in astrology. That wasn't the issue at all. It was not the responsibility or purpose of the HEC Board to either support or refute belief systems. Had we gone into the meeting defending astrology and proclaiming our "beliefs" about how and why it worked, or offered to do their charts to prove astrology's validity, we would have been shown the door. We had to first speak in THEIR language and understand THEIR criteria before an objective exchange could occur.

So what is the point of this story? By creating an academic program that included all core academic requirements of any degree granting college, we were prepared to meet and defend our program to the Higher Education Coordinating Board. And never, throughout the entire process, were we put in a position that caused us to soil the soul of astrology or alter the essence of the program we had created. In fact, the opposite is true. We only needed to speak in THEIR language so a relationship could be formed.

I now believe that astrology CAN integrate with other professions, and it can do that with no further delay. However, in order to do so, astrologers will be required to give up some their ideas about the importance of remaining "exclusive." Integration does not come out of segregation but rather it requires synthesis. Respect is not born in isolation.

Astrology belongs to everyone. Maybe it's time to give it to those to whom it really belongs. It was never really OURS to begin with. It rightfully belongs to THEM. By fighting to keep our autonomy as astrologers, are we inhibiting astrology itself? It is important that we honor the profession with which we want to participate, even if our ultimate intent is to reform it. It also requires us to demonstrate that we are knowledgeable about the profession we want to join.

Astrology is a "part" of everything. Perhaps we should stop defining it as a profession exclusive only to itself.

Astrology is unique in that it can be integrated with literally every profession. It complements, facilitates and helps us to better understand every area of life experience. Think for a moment of the benefits astrology could bring to literally every career. Consider, for example, the holistic health profession. It is unrealistic to believe that the holistic health community will open its doors to astrology unless astrologers are not only well-versed in astrology, but are also well-informed about holistic health. Astrology was part of a physicians training well into the 17th Century. Knowing that fact alone can lead to an interest in astrology in the holistic health areas. Still, education in the field will be prerequisite before astrology will be invited to merge with this profession.

If you hope to teach astrology in an academic setting, you must first have an academic degree. With the appropriate academic credentials, astrologers can begin to introduce astrology to their students and fellow teachers. It's already being done at several universities, even though astrology is not in the title of classes being taught. When astrologers who wish to teach in an academic setting first learn to speak the language of the academic community, then the academic community is more likely to understand the importance of what's being said.

But there is something else to consider here. Would a teacher who understands astrology and teaches it in an academic environment be called an astrologer or a teacher? By merging with a profession in the academic or any other professional field, everything starts to change. Astrology may no longer define the professional title, even though it is the subject being taught or used. Will astrology lose its power by merging with other professions, or will it regain its power by letting go of its autonomy and exclusivity?

Using another example, if you hope to bring astrology into the world of finance and show how astrological cycles correspond to celestial events, then you need to understand how the market works. In this environment, would you call yourself an astrologer? Or would you be a financial consultant who uses astrological techniques for predicting market changes? By merging astrology with an existing profession, your title will change, and with this change of title, your exclusivity as an astrologer is endangered. Could it be that we, as astrologers, are unconsciously afraid of losing our identities by merging with other professions? Is that fear, or our ego attachment to our title, actually holding astrology back from fulfilling its larger potential? Could it be that astrologers are astrology's worst enemy?

If you want to integrate astrology with the professional world, then you must allow the integration to occur and stop viewing astrology as a profession that must be separate from all others. Take the time to learn about the profession you want to join. Learn to speak in a language that is understood by that profession. Once you have established your expertise within the profession of your choice, be prepared to show evidence of the role astrology can play in its ultimate success. And whatever else you do, speak in a language that is familiar to the profession.

Kepler College of Astrological Arts & Sciences represents a major step forward in the quest to bring astrology to the professional world. We live in a world where academic degrees are important. Kepler College is the only college in the world that offers BA and MA degrees in astrological studies and brings astrology into its entire curriculum. When students learn about medical astrology they also learn about anatomy and critical issues in the health sciences. When they learn about financial astrology, they also study the world of finance. When they learn about astrology's role in the world of psychology, they learn psychology and counseling techniques. When they learn about history, astrology is included. The BA and MA degree programs are designed to meet academic requirements for a variety of professional fields. Kepler provides graduates with the academic requirements needed to move into the world and begin to integrate astrology with other fields of learning. Its graduates will not only be able to say, "I am an astrologer," they will be qualified to say, "I am a financial consultant who uses astrology," or. "I use astrological principles as a means of diagnosis," or, "I am a professional counselor. I use astrological principles to help people understand themselves." Astrology may no longer be the professional title, but instead it becomes an important ingredient in the profession that adds a new dimension to the field.

An academic degree in astrological studies, astrology and the health sciences, astrology and the counseling arts, etc., isn't right for everyone. There is certainly nothing wrong with being a good old-fashioned astrologer. However, by continuing to isolate astrology from other professions, I wonder if we are limiting astrology's potential to serve the larger world? By holding tightly to our beloved art/science and refusing to integrate it with other professions, are we keeping the world from acquiring the full benefits that astrology can offer. As long as we hold onto the belief that it is US versus THEM the full potential of astrology will never be realized. It is up to us to bring astrology to the masses, but we need to do it in a way that meets THEIR criteria. It can be done. It's being done. Astrology is growing up. We need to allow and to encourage it to move into the world and be all that it can be. We need to stop holding it back; we need to let it go and let it thrive; we need to stop "owning" it.

Like a mother who eventually needs to cut the apron strings and let her child move into the world, astrologers need to allow astrology freedom to meet the larger world and begin to integrate with it. In order to do that, I believe that WE need to integrate with THEM and allow astrology to become a part of the whole instead of an isolated study that is segregated from it.

* * * * *

Joanne Wickenburg has lectured extensively throughout the USA and Canada, and is the author of six books as well as a Correspondence Course in astrology. Joanne is a founding Board Member of Kepler College of Astrological Arts and Sciences and currently chairs the Board of Trustees. She is a recipient of the Marc Edmond Jones Award, and was a 1998 nominee for the Regulus Award in Education.

ETHICS TRAINING

by David Cochran, B.A., C.A.P.

ISAR (The International Society for Astrological Research) offers an astrological certification program. A person who fulfills the requirements for certification can use the initials C.A.P. (Certified Astrology Professional). In order to receive certification, the applicant must demonstrate a thorough knowledge of astrology by passing ISAR approved exams, demonstration of counseling skills, and an ISAR approved ethics training. ISAR offers an ethics training seminar for applicants who haven't attended an approved ethics training seminar elsewhere.

The purpose of ISAR's Ethics Seminar is to expose the astrological consultant to ethical dilemmas that arise in the counseling situation, and how other professions (psychologists, therapists, etc.) handle these issues. The Ethics Seminar sharpens your awareness and sensitivity to ethical issues that arise in the counseling situation, and prepares you to properly handle these situations.

A few of the key points made in the ISAR Ethics Seminar, and excerpted from the first version of the manual that was handed out to attendees of the first ISAR Ethics Seminar, are given below. The excerpts below are taken from the first part of the manual and address issues of what an astrologer's responsibilities are, limits to what an astrologer can ethically advise, and guidelines for ethical advertising.

Note that the ISAR ethics guidelines are exactly that: **GUIDELINES**. These guidelines are not designed to be hard and fast absolute commandments for astrologers. Each of us has our own personal ethical standards, and ISAR does not expect anyone to forfeit their own personal values in favor of an organizational standard. However, by presenting the astrologer with very specific and detailed ethical guidelines, the astrologer becomes more acutely aware of the many ethical issues that arise in their astrological practice and is given information on how other professions handle these issues. This exposure to ethical standards in other respected professions and the possible ways that one can conduct oneself in a responsible and professional manner are invaluable, and attendees of the seminar leave with much greater awareness, insight, and knowledge about professional standards, ethical problems, and ways in which to best conduct their professional practice.

Below are a few excerpts:

Astrologers' moral standards and conduct are personal matters to the same degree as is true for any other person, except that an astrologer's conduct may compromise their professional responsibilities or reduce the public's trust in astrology and astrologers. It is the individual responsibility of each astrologer to aspire to the highest possible standard of conduct.

As there are several sub-disciplines in astrology, a comprehensive code of ethics must endeavor to cover a variety of different situations. What is ethically relevant to a horary or financial astrologer may not apply to a counseling astrologer whose client is struggling with a relationship problem. This code, therefore, strives to recognize the specific ethical standards that apply in the different sub-disciplines of astrology. It also covers activities outside the field of counseling, such as interactions with the public, teaching, supervision, and research. We recognize that the development of standards is an ongoing process and that this code is a living document subject to revisions and updates as needed.

Every conceivable situation that may occur cannot be expressly covered by this code. The absence of a specific prohibition against a particular kind of conduct does not mean that such conduct is ethical. Accordingly, while the specific wording of these standards is important, the spirit and intent of the principles should always be taken into consideration by those utilizing or interpreting this code.

Adherence to a dynamic set of ethical standards requires a personal commitment to a life-long effort to act ethically; to encourage ethical behavior by one's colleagues; and to consult with others, as needed, concerning ethical problems.

Primary Responsibility

The prime directive that supercedes all other ethics is *do no harm.* Astrologers act at all times in the client's best interest. Given below are excerpts from the ISAR Ethics Code. These excerpts were selected with assistance from the rest of the ISAR board. They present some of the most important concepts and were carefully selected so that they are complete and easily readable out of the context of the rest of the ISAR Ethics Code.

A.3. Personal Needs and Values
    a. *Personal Needs*

        Astrologers are aware of the intimacy and responsibilities inherent in the counseling relationship, maintain respect for clients, and avoid actions that seek to meet their personal needs at the expense of clients.

    b. *Personal Values*

        Astrologers are aware of their own values, attitudes, and beliefs, realize that we live in a diverse society, and avoid imposing their values on clients.

A.4. Respecting Diversity

    a. *Nondiscrimination*

        Astrologers do not discriminate against clients, students, or supervisees in a manner that has a negative impact based on their age, color, culture, disability, ethnic group, gender, race, religion, sexual orientation, marital status, or socioeconomic status, or for any other reason.

    b. *Respecting Differences*

        Astrologers will actively attempt to understand the diverse cultural backgrounds of the clients with whom they work. This includes, but is not limited to, learning how the astrologer's own cultural/ethnic/racial identity impacts his/her values and beliefs about the counseling process.

A.5. Professional Competence

    a. *Boundaries of Competence*

        Astrologers practice only within the boundaries of their competence, based on their education, training, supervised experience, and appropriate professional experience.

    b. *New Specialty Areas of Practice*

        Astrologers practice in specialty areas new to them only after appropriate education, training, and supervised experience. While developing skills in new specialty areas, astrologers take steps to ensure the competence of their work and to protect others from possible harm.

c. *Monitor Effectiveness*

Astrologers continually monitor their effectiveness as professionals and take steps to improve when necessary. Astrologers take reasonable steps to seek out peer supervision to evaluate their efficacy as astrologers.

d. *Ethical Issues Consultation*

Astrologers take reasonable steps to consult with other counselors or related professionals when they have questions regarding their ethical obligations or professional practice.

e. *Continuing Education*

Astrologers recognize the need for continuing education to maintain a reasonable level of awareness of current scientific and professional information in their fields of activity. This may include attending conferences, taking courses, and studying literature. Astrologers take steps to maintain competence in the skills they use and are open to new procedures.

f. *Impairment*

Astrologers refrain from rendering professional services when their physical, mental, or emotional problems are likely to harm a client or others. They are alert to signs of impairment, seek assistance for problems, and, if necessary, limit, suspend, or terminate their professional responsibilities.

A.6. Advertising and Soliciting Clients
  a. *Definition*
      Advertising entails, but is not limited to, all paid and unpaid statements in media, brochures, business cards, direct mail promotions, directory listings, resumes, and other printed matter. Advertising also includes statements made in oral presentations such as lectures and classes, as well as comments for use in electronic media such as television, radio, and the Internet.
  b. *Accurate Advertising*
      It is unethical for astrologers to make false, fraudulent, misleading, or deceptive claims that are designed to induce the rendering of professional services. A statement may be misleading or deceptive if it fails to disclose material facts or is intended or is likely to create false or unjustified expectations of favorable results.

* * * * *

David Cochran is a full-time computer programmer for Cosmic Patterns Software. David pioneered some new theories of astrological interpretation using harmonics and midpoints in the 1970's. From 1973 to 1980, David was a full-time practicing astrologer, and around 1980 he dropped his astrological practice to devote full-time to developing astrological software.

During the 1970's David developed a unique and comprehensive system of chart interpretation based primarily on harmonic theory. David synthesized ideas from cosmobiology, harmonics, Vedic astrology, and other areas into an integrated system to interpret astrology charts. During the past 10 years he has refined the system, and included features in the Kepler program that aid in applying these theories and using them practically in astrological consultations.

David was born May 1, 1949, at 4:26 AM in East Meadow, New York (time zone 5 hours west, daylight savings time observed). He has a BA degree in psychology, and C.A.P. certification. He is currently also serving as President of ISAR (International Society for Astrological Research).

THE IMPORTANCE OF PEER GROUPS

by Arlan Wise

A peer group is a group of professional consulting astrologers who meet to discuss clients and consultations that have been problematical. It is a meeting of peers to discuss client issues. The consultation may have been difficult, brought up questions about counseling technique or times when you've felt you've done a bad job. It is a safe place to share problems and look for the underlying motives and meanings of what happened in the consultation that made you feel disturbed. It is a safe place to discuss feelings, vent frustrations, and ask for help and guidance. And tell interesting stories.

Purpose

Peer group work grounds us and lets the input of other astrologers act as a reality check. It is an opportunity to give and receive support among other professional astrologers. We can share practical advice and ideas. It gives us a chance to let our unconscious material become apparent to others whom we trust and who can point these issues out to us. We can see through the discussion if it was the client or our own work that was the problem. We can discuss feelings of failure and inadequacy. We have a place to discuss those difficult clients. This is the only place we can break client confidentiality to talk about our clients.

Our peers can help us see how we complicate the problem. We discuss what works and doesn't work in the consultation. Peer group work is of tremendous benefit to those astrologers who are beginning their consulting practice. It is helpful for them to see that experienced astrologers also have problems and doubts about their work.

There is no blame or judgment. We focus on how we can help each other do better work. By relating the story of the disturbing consultation, we can see how we have become entangled in the client's story and lost our objective perspective. Often when we get sucked into the story, some issue of our own is being triggered. The group can help give a psychological perspective on where we are entering the consultation in an in appropriate manner. They help us to see where our own stuff is bleeding through, where we may not be aware of a hidden bias or prejudice.

Peer group work is not about learning astrology. It is assumed that that is known. Peer work addresses how to use the astrology of the client to solve consulting problems. We can see the dynamics of the client but do not spend the time delineating his/her chart. This is not the place to learn astrology techniques although that happens as an adjunct from the discussions. The tips and jewels you learn by listening to your fellow astrologers is one of the perks. But, peer group is not a place to show off interpretation skills. The chart is used as a reference to help understand why the astrologer had difficulties with this one.

The bottom line purpose of peer group work is to help us do better consultations.

How to Create a Peer Group

The underlying model is the therapeutic one. Therapists, social workers, psychiatrists all do peer work. There are only two strict rules: 1. No one uses the names of the clients. 2. Everything that is said in the meeting is confidential. Nothing leaves the room.

I belong to a group in Boston that has been running for 6 years. We were started by Michael Lutin who gave a course on client work. He taught day-long workshops in psychoanalytic techniques for a year and a half. He taught us to listen to the language of the unconscious and then he left us on our own. We have evolved our own style, as each group will do. Each group will develop differently according to the members involved.

We have found that a group of 6 to14 works best although 2 or 3 astrologers could do a fine job. It depends on who can gather together. We meet one afternoon a month at the leader's house. We set the first Friday of the month as the date to make it easy to remember. We break for the summer months and invite new members to join when we start up in September. Once the group is formed, it is better not to add new members. But, you can also do it the way that works best for you. We start with a potluck lunch. This gives us a chance to gossip, exchange news, talk about everything besides clients. After lunch we move into the living room and then the talk is focused on clients. Members bring clients' charts, with the names cut off, and give each one in the group a copy. The presenter gives an outline of the consultation and says what has bothered him/her about the consultation. We will have a discussion in which group members ask questions that help the astrologer presenting the case to gain insight into the situation. When the discussion is over, the presenter tries to summarize what s/he learned and how s/he was helped. The issue needs to be one that is real, a hot issue for the presenter, something important and something that feels unresolved.

It is useful to have a leader to keep the discussion centered and focused on the chart under discussion. The leader can rein in tangents and keep returning to the topics. The leader can also be directive if one person is talking too much or just filling the space with words. Each member who wishes should have the chance to speak. Once the discussion begins to be on topics not relevant to the chart or presenter, than the discussion is finished. You can also see this when people start to leave the room, usually to go to the bathroom. There is no time limit to the individual discussions. We usually work in a peer group session for 3 to 3 1/2 hours.

This is fluid work and resists a strict structure. There needs to be trust among the members and a feeling of safety must be built. No one is allowed to criticize or attack each other. It is important to be aware of the group dynamics and try to identify if anyone is taking on a role, i.e., the boss, the saboteur, the observer, the needy one. Quite often there are indications of an unconscious sibling rivalry occurring between astrologers. Personal control issues and other psychological issues do arise, and the group helps the member become aware of why s/he may be saying what s/he says. We act as observers and help each other to recognize where we may be stuck in patterns in our consulting style. We point out where the astrologer is the recipient of the client's projection.

As I said, there are no rules except not to mention the names of clients and to keep total confidentiality. (That is the reason there are no stories to illustrate this text.) There is no cost for the meeting as we meet in someone's home. If there were a need to rent a space then the group members would share the rent. All techniques of astrology (western, Vedic, horary, classical) are fine; that doesn't matter since it is the consultation and the consultation problems that are the focus. We also help with practical issues, setting up one's frame of work, setting boundaries for fees and time, tape recorders and referrals.

This is valuable work, and OPA is trying to encourage our members to begin local peer groups. We will be giving workshops on peer work at our conferences so that members may experience the bonding that occurs as a group of professional astrologers focus on helping a colleague. It needs to be experienced, so I urge all of you reading this to give it a try and form a group composed of astrologers in your local area, and then start to meet once a month. You'll be glad you did.

* * * * *

Arlan Wise has worked as a professional consulting astrologer since 1979. She maintains a practice on Martha's Vineyard, MA, where she lives. She writes an astrology column for the Martha's Vineyard Times. She loves to teach. Arlan served for four years as the Newsletter Editor of the Career Astrologer. She is presently the Vice President/Membership Secretary of OPA.